G000041312

FROM BAGS
TO BLENDERS

FROM BAGS TO BLENDERS

The Journey of a Yorkshire Businessman

GORDON
BLACK

This edition published in the UK in 2017 by
Icon Books Ltd, Omnibus Business Centre,
39–41 North Road, London N7 9DP
email: info@iconbooks.com
www.iconbooks.com

First published in the UK in 2016 by Icon Books Ltd

Sold in the UK, Europe and Asia
by Faber & Faber Ltd, Bloomsbury House,
74–77 Great Russell Street,
London WC1B 3DA or their agents

Distributed in the UK, Europe and Asia
by Grantham Book Services,
Trent Road, Grantham NG31 7XQ

Distributed in Australia and New Zealand
by Allen & Unwin Pty Ltd,
PO Box 8500, 83 Alexander Street,
Crows Nest, NSW 2065

Distributed in South Africa by
Jonathan Ball, Office B4, The District,
41 Sir Lowry Road, Woodstock 7925

Distributed in India by Penguin Books India,
7th Floor, Infinity Tower – C, DLF Cyber City,
Gurgaon 122002, Haryana

ISBN: 978-178578-204-6

Text copyright © 2016 Gordon Black
The author has asserted his moral rights

No part of this book may be reproduced in any form, or by any
means, without prior permission in writing from the publisher

Typeset by Simmons Pugh
Cover design by Sam Oakes of Gobo Systems
Printed and bound in the UK by Clays Ltd, St Ives plc

Contents

About the Author   6

Introduction   7

Monetary Values   11

Chapter One   Brief History   14

Chapter Two   Three Stages   41

Chapter Three   Leadership   56

Chapter Four   Arrogance   75

Chapter Five   Product   82

Chapter Six   Good Business Practice is
                     Enlightened Self-Interest   92

Chapter Seven   Timing   106

Chapter Eight   Balance   114

Chapter Nine   High Street TV   124

Chapter Ten   Conclusion   130

Index   145

About the author

Gordon Black CBE DL was born in 1943 and educated at Bootham School, York and Clare College, Cambridge, where he took a degree in History.

He joined Peter Black in 1965 and became Chairman in 1977. Peter Black Holdings was a major supplier of footwear, toiletries, cosmetics, pharmaceuticals and logistics to the UK's leading retailers, with annual sales of £300 million and around 3,000 employees. It was a plc for 25 years and was then taken private in 2000. The remaining companies were sold to Li & Fung, a Hong Kong-based global trading company, in 2007.

Gordon Black now runs Black Family Investments with his brother Thomas, and was awarded a CBE in 2005 for services to business and charity. He is married to Louise, with three children and nine grandchildren, and lives in Yorkshire.

This book is dedicated to my wife, Louise, and my family.

INTRODUCTION

This book has been a challenge from the beginning to the end. Even choosing a title has been problematic. The working title was *What I Have Learnt*. As I view arrogance as a cardinal sin, it dawned on me that this title was somewhat presumptuous as I have not finished learning. Someone suggested *Black & Blue*. Perhaps this was a reference to the fact that on a long, rollercoaster business ride one can get bruised from time to time. One of the less salubrious members of my family came up with *Fifty Shades of Black*. This one did appeal as I certainly do not want to be taken too seriously and it would have boosted sales. However, it had to be binned as I would have risked seriously disappointing my readers. *From Bags to Riches* was voted out as it was considered not to be in good taste and not entirely accurate. I considered *Work in Progress*. Then I thought this was a little optimistic for a man of more than three score years and ten. I finally settled on *From Bags to Blenders*. Shopping bags were the first product my father manufactured when he started the business in 1947. The Nutribullet blender was a blockbuster game changer at High Street TV, which was the last company in which I have been involved.

I have tried to analyse why I am actually putting pen to paper. In a way, it is cathartic, in that I am dismayed by some of the goings-on in business today and therefore I have a strong urge to get my views off my chest. I also feel a sense of closure in that my days of writing reports and making speeches are coming to an end. In addition I want to express my pride in what my parents achieved in the face of adversity, and my appreciation of the start in life they gave to my brother, Thomas, my sister, Josefine, and myself. My main motivation is to pass on to my family, friends and anyone who is interested the lessons I have learnt and the observations I have made in a long and action-packed business career.

There have been many books published in recent times about eminent retailers. Rarely has anyone written without constraint about the reality of supplying retailers, as they are frightened of the repercussions.

I am aware my style of writing is more *Daily Mail* than *Times Literary Supplement* and it will certainly offend the purists. Reading through what I have written confirms to me that I am not a natural author. It reflects my background in that much of it reads more like an essay or the transcript of a speech. In addition, I am aware that I do tend to repeat myself (my wife will think this is the understatement of the year) and I am sure that some of my hackneyed phrases ('low hanging fruit'; 'the global economy is a reality') will make some of those who know me groan somewhat. There have been many amusing incidents that have occurred over the years. I have woven various anecdotes into the narrative, and hopefully this will make the book a lighter reading experience. I am told that the average novel is about 80,000 words while my literary effort is about 32,000 words. The fact that this is a short book might make you think I have not learnt much. I would prefer you to react positively to this brevity, as I have worked hard to avoid jargon and waffle and to be succinct.

I certainly do not aim to cause offence. I am proud to be a Yorkshireman. Our trademark is bluntness – we tend to call a spade a shovel. I hope this outspoken approach will be viewed as forthright rather than arrogant – they say 'you can tell a Yorkshireman, but you can't tell him much!' I do hope my views will be accepted in the positive spirit intended.

Absolutely everything I have been involved with has been very much a team effort. My most sincere thanks therefore go to all the great colleagues I have worked with over the years for their support, loyalty and friendship. I want to express my special appreciation to my wife Louise, my brother Thomas, and to Dick Leivers and Stephen Lister, who were both Managing Directors of Peter Black and made an immense contribution to the development of the business. I also want to thank Andrew Malcher and Jim Coleman, the founders of High Street TV, and my PA, Alison

Whitham. I am grateful to Peter Pugh of Icon Books whose input and patience enabled this literary project to get over the line.

I have enjoyed reading several books by well-known businessmen which are packed with reminiscences and character assassinations. As I never kept a diary, and I cannot remember too much detail from the past, I have chosen a different approach. While there are certainly many stories about the Black family to relate, the emphasis is more analytical than biographical. In addition I appreciate that many people will never have heard about Peter Black. My first chapter will therefore run through the history of the company in order to provide a backcloth to what will follow.

As you will gather, any success we have had has been based on the fact that we made more good decisions than bad, but only just.

Monetary Values

Money and its value is always a problem when writing about a period that stretches over a number of years, particularly when parts of that period have included some years of very high inflation. Furthermore, establishing a yardstick for measuring the change in the value of money is not easy either. Do we take the external value of the £ or what it will buy in the average (whatever that may be) weekly shopping basket? Do we relate it to the average manual wage? As we know, while prices in general might rise, and have done so in this country every year since the Second World War, the prices of certain products might fall. However, we are writing about a business, and money and its value crop up on several pages. We therefore have to make some judgements. We can only generalise, and I think the best yardstick is probably the average working wage.

Taking this as the yardstick, here is a measure of the £ sterling relative to the £ in 2016.

Apart from wartime, prices were stable for 250 years,

but began to rise in the run-up to the First World War.

1665–1900 multiply by 120
1900–1914 multiply by 110
1918–1939 multiply by 60
(*In Germany there was a period of hyperinflation in the early 1920s*)
1945–1950 multiply by 35
1950–1960 multiply by 30
1960–1970 multiply by 25
1970–1974 multiply by 20
1975–1977 multiply by 15
1978–1980 multiply by 8
1980–1987 multiply by 5
1987–1991 multiply by 2.5
1991–1997 multiply by 2

Since 1997, the rate of inflation, by the standards of most of the 20th century, has been very low, averaging, until very recently, less than the government's originally stated aim of 2.5 per cent (since reduced to 2 per cent). Some things such as telephone charges and many items made in the Far East, notably China, are going down in price while others, such as houses, moved up very sharply from 1997 to 2008 before falling back in the financial crisis. In 2011 on the back of sharply rising commodity and food prices, inflation accelerated again to reach 5 per cent per annum. However, as commodity prices fell back and much of the world suffered very low growth, the rate of inflation began to subside again in 2012 and 2013. Indeed, by 2016 many of the industrialised nations are starting to worry about deflation.

CHAPTER ONE

BRIEF HISTORY

Both my parents were born in Germany. My father's name was Hans Schwarzschild and his family were patrons of the arts and academics. His uncle, Karl Schwarzschild, was a famous astronomer and a friend of Einstein. My mother's name was Else Kohlmann and her family were the largest cigar manufacturers in Germany. Hans was brought up in Frankfurt and apparently was a rather shy but tidy and well organised boy who made his brother sign in and out for his toys – clearly a sign for what was to follow! His father's family business was Dick & Goldschmidt which was a well-known global textile trading company. His brother, Paul, went into the family business and Hans joined a company which manufactured leather goods (briefcases, handbags etc.). My father met my mother at a language school in Frankfurt. Mercifully my parents were perceptive and, foreseeing the horrors of Hitler's Nazi regime, fled to England in 1935.

It is important to relate briefly the background to the emergence of Hitler and the persecution of the Jews. In the early 20th century the Jews in Germany were well integrated into society. Many fought in the First World War and were generally successful and well respected. Germany's defeat in November 1918 led to escalating economic problems for the country. In order to pay for the large costs of the war, Germany had suspended the Gold Standard and resorted to borrowing. This strategy backfired when Germany lost the war and was faced with a massive war debt. France and Britain demanded high annual repayments of the reparations dictated at the Treaty of Versailles in 1919 and this led to a rapid decline in the value of the German mark and escalating inflation.

By the autumn of 1922 Germany found itself unable to make reparations payments and by this time the mark was virtually worthless. Inflation was exacerbated when workers in the Ruhr went on strike and the government printed more money to continue paying them for their 'passive resistance'. By November 1923 one American dollar was worth 4,210,500,000 German marks. The effect on the German people was appalling and this hyperinflation can be seen as one of the causes of the rise of Adolf Hitler.

The Nazi Party's rise to power, and Adolf Hitler's appointment by Hindenberg as the German Chancellor on 30 January 1933, had catastrophic effects for Jews in Germany. Hitler scheduled new elections to a 'bogus' Reichstag on 5 March 1933, he intimidated his opponents, and a week before the election the Reichstag itself went up in flames, possibly at the hands of the Nazis. That was the beginning. The rest followed in rapid succession. Jewish-owned shops were boycotted, Jews were expelled from the National Academy and from government positions, schools, research institutes and universities. They were banned from practising law and other professions and excluded from all national societies. A few weeks in spring 1933 sufficed to reduce the University of Göttingen, a world-renowned centre of advanced physics and mathematics, to the level of a provincial college.

The passing of the Nuremberg Laws in 1935 excluded Jews from many jobs, made it illegal for them to marry 'Aryans' and established them as second-class citizens. What had brought such anti-Semitic feeling to be so widely acceptable within Germany, within a land in which the Jews, including the Schwarzchilds, had felt at home and prospered, had even contributed to? A major tenet of the Nazi propaganda machine was that the Jewish people had contributed to Germany's defeat in 1918, and were involved in the social and economic problems that the country had faced since the end of the First World War.

My parents arrived in London penniless and rented a one-room basement flat. My father got a job with the London branch of the company he worked for in Germany. With the advent of war he was asked by his employer to locate and run a small production unit outside London to manufacture army webbing (belts, and ammunition holders). After an exhaustive search he found a vacant floor in an old textile mill in Keighley, West Yorkshire.

His deep gratitude to this country for giving him refuge, and his appreciation of the warm welcome extended to him in Keighley, were behind his determination to integrate fully and to become as much an Englishman as possible. He changed his name from Hans Schwarzschild to Peter Black; he never spoke German at home; Thomas and I were sent away at a young age to boarding school; and he tried to understand the intricacies of cricket. The name change did cause some confusion. The literal translation of Schwarzschild into English is Black Shield. PB, as my father became known, and his brother decided to split the name – we became the Blacks and my Uncle Paul's family became the Shields. To add to the confusion, my grandmother retained the original name. PB used to tell the story of when he met his brother and mother at a restaurant in London for dinner. He said to the unfortunate receptionist, 'I'm Mr Black, are my brother Mr Shields and my mother Mrs Schwarzschild here yet?'

In a previous publication about the family, my brother Thomas wrote the following about my parents:

Peter Black was not an easy man to live with and, if he provided the brains and flair of the outfit, my mother provided the toughness. She was busy running the home and, while was not interested in the specifics of the business, she was very supportive. In all the traditional ways she was an elegant asset to Peter Black, who had high standards, and, like her husband, she was proud to be British. She integrated into the community and was very popular. She loved crosswords and Scrabble, embracing the English language even if she struggled with the English 'w', thus pronouncing Wimbledon, Watford and Willesden with a 'v'.

After the war, with the help of a financial backer, Peter Black bought the production unit in Keighley from his London-based employer. He used the surplus webbing material to manufacture shopping bags. His first customers were Marks & Spencer and Boots. With considerable imagination and courage, he then went to the Gold Coast (now Ghana) and sold containers full of bags to the Bata Organisation, an international trading company originating in Czechoslovakia.

In the early 1950s, the traditional slipper business was transformed by the development of vulcanising – a method of heat-bonding a light rubber sole to a fabric upper. Marks & Spencer's footwear manufacturers did not have the sewing capacity to keep up with demand. This led Marks & Spencer to ask PB to sew some uppers for their main supplier. It did not take him long to realise that it would be a good idea to invest in vulcanising machinery and become a slipper supplier himself. In order to get a strong bond between the sole and the upper, traditional slipper manufacturers using the vulcanising process limited themselves to smooth-surfaced textile materials. Although corduroy was a big fashion, it was not considered suitable to be used for uppers on vulcanised slippers on account of the ridges in the fabric. PB addressed and overcame the problem. We were the first to produce corduroy slippers, which proved to be a fast seller. This was the opportunistic beginning of our footwear business, which at its peak supplied over 20 million pairs per year to the leading retailers in the UK and abroad.

My brother Thomas, born in November 1938, is four years older than I am. He married Sue Broughton in 1967 and they have four sons, Adam, Ben, Oliver, and Daniel. Along with my wife, Thomas has always been my best friend and also business partner. After National Service (two years in the army), Thomas trained with Marks & Spencer and then worked in factories abroad before joining the company in 1962. While working for Marks & Spencer on the shop floor in their Leeds store, there was an incident Thomas has never forgotten. The manager told him that if he saw anyone he recognised (meaning senior executives from Marks & Spencer head office in London) he should introduce himself, give them the latest sales information and then take them for a coffee to the staff dining room. Half way through Thomas's second week, a well-dressed gentleman came into the store and smiled at Thomas. In line with his instructions, Thomas introduced himself, explained at length how each department was trading and then proceeded with his guest to the staff dining room for a coffee. Thomas was puzzled by the bemused expression on his guest's face. Then the penny dropped. He was entertaining the head barman from the Devonshire Arms Hotel at Bolton Abbey!

I read History at Cambridge – my father always joked that it was as close to Footwear as he could find. After university, I also trained at Marks & Spencer, spent six months in an accountancy firm and worked in factories in Europe and America before joining Peter Black full time at the age of 22 in 1965. My time at Marks & Spencer was also not incident-free. Initially, I was placed at their Wembley store. On my first morning the manager gave me a stern lecture along the lines that 70 per cent of the employees were girls and he did not welcome illicit liaisons. I was young and naive. It took me a few weeks to realise that I was the only one taking any notice of the manager's directive. From Wembley, I was transferred to the head office in Baker Street, where I was attached (not literally) to the Ladies' Underwear Buying Department.

In his later years, Peter Black spent much of his time building up a collection of veteran and vintage cars. His motivation was two-fold. First, he had always been interested in cars. He must have inherited this interest from his uncle, who had a factory in Camden Town in London which produced a car called the Sabella between 1908 and 1912. (We actually have the remains of a Sabella in our collection.) Secondly, he was scarred by living through the hyperinflation in Germany when they printed money and you had to collect your wages with a wheelbarrow. He consequently distrusted any form of paper money, including shares. He preferred palpable assets.

Sadly, my father's health deteriorated in the months prior to his death at the age of 69 in 1977. Despite his illness, he maintained an active interest in the company's performance. The most important time of the week for him was late on Friday afternoon when our turnover for the week was printed out. I will never forget one Friday in late March 1977. My father was very ill in St Mary's Hospital in London. We got the call that the end was nigh. Thomas and I rushed to London and, like in the films, the whole family was assembled around my father's bed. He appeared to be in a coma. To our amazement, at 4.00pm he opened his eyes and said, 'Have you got the turnover?' and then immediately went back to sleep. Thomas and I agreed that, as it was probably his last turnover, he should die happy and we therefore made up some highly inflated figures. At 5.00pm his eyes opened again, we told him the turnover and he said 'excellent' and went back to sleep. A week later, he made a remarkable recovery and gave Thomas and me a royal ticking off for giving him inaccurate information. He lived for another six months.

In the early 1970s the business entered a prolonged period of steady expansion. In 1970 we employed around 400 people and had annual sales of £2 million (£50 million in today's money). In 1990 we had over 4,000 employees and operated from 34 locations in the UK and overseas. Annual sales were over £250 million (over £600 million today).

In 1972 we successfully took the business public. We travelled first class in that we were advised by Cazenove, and Rothschild was our merchant bank. Founded in 1823 by Philip Cazenove, Cazenove was the quintessential City stockbroker and was one of the UK's last independent investment brokers to remain a private partnership. It was well-known for its blue-blooded reputation and aversion to publicity. A friend of my children, many years ago, did a few weeks' work experience there in a summer vacation. The weather was unusually hot and there was no air-conditioning in the office. Our friend asked his superior if it was all right to take his jacket off. Only at Cazenove would one get the following reply: 'Potatoes have jackets, gentlemen wear coats.'

Given his dislike for shares, PB was lukewarm about the whole process. He did, however, insist that, for historic reasons, we used the merchant bank, NM Rothschild. Rothschild translated into English means Red Shield. In the 18th century the Red Shields were neighbours of the Black Shields in a famous street in Frankfurt. Sadly, they did rather better than us – they went into banking and we went into footwear. I was given the responsibility of getting the deal over the line.

At the age of 29, it was quite a daunting task. However, I learnt a lot and the experience stood me in good stead for what was to follow.

The Times had this to say about the flotation in January 1972:

[Peter Black] ... is a substantial supplier of Marks & Spencer ... [but the flotation] will hardly set the market alight. Rothschild is offering 1.4 million shares which equals 35 per cent of the equity. At 105p therefore the capitalisation is £4.2 million [£84 million in today's money]. This raises no new money but helps the spending of £500,000 [£10 million] on fixed assets over the last three years. The arrival of two sons in the business provided the impetus.

In the eight years to 1969–70 turnover expanded from £1.6 million to £3.7 million [£23 million to £74 million]. Pre-tax margins averaged 7 per cent. In the year to April 1971 sales rose to £4.7 million [£94 million] and margins improved to 9 per cent with profits jumping 63 per cent to £427,000 [£8.5 million] putting the shares on a price-earnings ratio of 13.3 at 105p.

The price looks modest but it must be remembered that the company is dependent on three customers – Marks & Spencer at 41 per cent, British Shoe at 14 per cent and Boots at 11 per cent. The major factory is at Keighley but a shortage of local machinists has meant the farming out of production to four small factories.

In the event the shares immediately rose and proved to be a good investment for many of our employees who took advantage of a preferential right to subscribe – £100 invested in 1972 was worth over £2,500 in the year 2000 when we took the business private again.

The principal milestones on our journey of expansion were:

Peter Black Footwear & Accessories

Offices in Italy and the Far East

The opening of our offices in Italy and the Far East was certainly one of the most important milestones on the Peter Black journey. It was nothing like as straight-forward or simple as one might think. A founding principle of Marks & Spencer, our largest customer, was to buy British. In every store there was a big sign stating that 99 per cent of their products were British made. There was a clear commercial logic behind this patriotism – the more people employed in their suppliers' factories, the more consumer spending potential there would be to buy Marks & Spencer products in their stores. In the late 1970s, it was clear that the world was changing. An increasing amount of products which had a high sewing labour content, such as bags and footwear, was coming from Asia, where wages were significantly lower than in Europe. Against this background, the challenge was to reconcile this reality with a cornerstone of Marks &

Spencer's philosophy. As Marks & Spencer developed their footwear offer, there was an appreciation that Italy had the best design and manufacturing skills for certain types of fashion shoe. We met this demand by buying a small company that had a sourcing office in Florence. To supply Marks & Spencer with imported products PB had to get permission and show M&S that the products were not available in the UK.

The Marks & Spencer buying departments had a frustrating dilemma. They appreciated the need to source globally but they were aware that this would need a fundamental change of policy which was not possible without main board approval. David Sieff, the son of Lord Sieff, was the director in charge of the footwear and bag buying departments. In November 1979, I went with David to New York to look at the shops. I remember what followed so clearly. Over dinner at the Waldorf Astoria, we discussed the Asian issue in depth. David was onside and we decided on the following course of action.

Bags, compared with clothing, were a low-profile product. I was to go to Asia, produce some samples and write a justification paper which David would present to the board. Prior to joining Peter Black full time, Thomas and I had spent a few months in Trenton, New Jersey, with a large manufacturer of bags and luggage. This company had been taken over by a firm called Airways which had opened offices in Korea, Hong Kong and China and whose head office was near Pittsburgh, Pennsylvania. We made an agreement with Airways which allowed us to use their offices in Asia. On 21 January 1980 I undertook a Jules Verne challenge – I went around the world in 14 days – Yorkshire to London; London to New York; New York to Pittsburgh; Pittsburgh to LA; LA to Tokyo; Tokyo to Seoul, Korea; Seoul to Taipan, Taiwan; Taipan to Hong Kong; Hong Kong to Singapore; Singapore to London. The sample bag I brought back was called an Organiser – a ladies' shoulder bag with numerous pockets. The basic argument of my justification paper which won the day was that we would not countenance any imported product which could be sourced competitively in the UK – we would therefore not be taking away orders and jobs from British factories. The rest is history. Our bags were the first products manufactured in Asia to be sold in Marks & Spencer. The business boomed. Footwear and clothing followed the same course. In 2007, Peter Black Distribution (the stand-alone logistics company we set up in the mid-1990s) had a contract with Marks & Spencer to process 50 million units of clothing per week from Asia. On a personal level, David Sieff became a close friend. Whenever we get together, we talk about the historic dinner at the Waldorf Astoria.

Bags

Necessity was the mother of invention! Shopping in the 1950s and 1960s was very different from today. There were very few supermarkets and shopping centres. People bought their food from individual grocers, butchers and bakers on the high street. Every household had shopping bags. The emergence of major supermarkets and the increasing ownership of cars triggered a dramatic change in shopping habits. The supermarkets gave customers free polythene carriers which caused the death of the traditional shopping bag. We used our manufacturing skill set to diversify into soft luggage, sports bags, toilet bags, and carrycots and prams for Mothercare, a chain of shops set up to cater for expectant mothers and children up to eight years old. The founder, Chairman and Chief Executive of Mothercare was Selim Zilkha. We observed in the United States the amazing success of Avon Cosmetics. We did some research and discovered that the bags their agents in the UK were using were imported from America. We got hold of a bag and made up a sample using material sourced from a friend who had a local weaving mill. I then took our bag to the Avon UK Head Office in Northampton. Our price was very competitive and we got a contract for 5,000 bags per week. This lasted for five years until Avon started buying the bag from Asia. We had a similar success with a hairdryer case for Ronson. Also, through our office in Hong Kong, we developed a range of handbags and accessories which proved to be very successful with Marks & Spencer and other leading retailers.

Footwear

The market for slippers went into decline principally for two reasons: First, there was the emergence of fitted carpets and the demise of the outside toilet, and second, the development of new ranges of gift products which threatened the position of slippers as a traditional Christmas present. This downturn was more than compensated for by an exciting development at Marks & Spencer. Until the early 1970s, Marks & Spencer's main business was the retailing of clothing. In the early 1970s, under the leadership of Marcus Sieff, they started giving increased priority to food and what they called 'non-clothing' which included footwear and accessories. We were well placed to take advantage of the new opportunities. We invested in the development of men's, ladies and children's formal, sports and leisure footwear. This was achieved by increasing production capacity in the UK, a few small but strategic acquisitions and, most importantly, by developing ranges through our offices in Italy and the Far East.

Peter Black Leisurewear

My brother and I have always loved sport, and I suppose there was a subconscious pull for us to find a way of incorporating this passion into our business lives. Slightly naively, we bought a small sports company that sold football boots and clothing. Very quickly we realised that if we did not invest substantial funds in sponsorship deals like the major brands, we would be an insignificant 'rat in the race'. From our travels abroad, we saw that the Adidas brand was less prevalent in the UK than in Europe. This observation was a eureka moment. We had spotted a gap in the market. Adidas already had an established distributor for the sports shops in the UK. We negotiated a deal with the Dassler family, who were the owners of Adidas, whereby we set up Peter Black Leisurewear, which had the right to distribute Adidas footwear and clothing to everyone other than sports shops, i.e. department stores, shoe shops and mail order. We also secured the rights for our manufacturing division to produce Adidas bags for the UK market. Sales went through the roof.

The Adidas story is a fascinating one. The name is derived from the founder:

Adolf Dassler → Adi Dassler → Adidas

Adi Dassler, in partnership with his brother, Rudolph Dassler, started after the Second World War manufacturing sports footwear in the small town of Herzogenaurach near Nuremberg. The two brothers fell out and Rudi crossed the river in the town and started a similar business called Puma. The rivalry between the two brothers was a motivating force for both companies. Thomas and I often joked that we might have done better if one of us had crossed the River Aire in Keighley and started up in Riddlesden.

The Dassler family were a strong management team – Adi was the technician, Mrs Dassler was very much the head of the family and the business, and their son Horst was a brilliant marketeer and strategist. I got on well with Horst from our first meeting. Until we arrived on the scene, Adidas had only sold worldwide through the sports trade. It was Horst who persuaded his mother to allow us to break the mould and supply multiple retailers. Following our successful launch, similar deals were set up all over the world.

Adidas had two head offices – one at Herzogenaurach and the other at Landersheim, near Strasbourg in France. Both were most impressive set-ups with modern offices, sports facilities and hotel-type accommodation. It was here that Adidas entertained the elite of the sporting world. For a young man whose horizons had been largely limited to making footwear and bags in Keighley, the visits to Adidas were an eye-opener to say the least. It was an enormous thrill to meet many leading international sportsmen and to observe the politics involved. We learnt so much about brand management and the use of PR and marketing. I did not let on that I spoke reasonably fluent French and a little German, as a result of which I sometimes heard more than they intended. An important lesson I learnt was *in vino veritas* – it is dangerous to drink too much at lavish dinners as alcohol certainly loosens the tongue, and the next morning one regrets the indiscretions of the previous evening. There was an incident when we were negotiating our initial deal with Adidas when my ability to bluff was seriously put to the test. Negotiations had gone well, and before we actually signed the contract I was invited to the Dassler home for dinner with the family, including Mr and Mrs Dassler Senior. I realised it was important that I made a good impression. I hate frogs' legs and snails and had managed to avoid eating them even when I lived in France for six months prior to going to university. Imagine my reaction when snails were dished up for the first course. I had a double challenge! First, I had to pretend I liked them. Secondly, I had to find instantly the technique of getting the little devils out of their shells. I managed it, just, and the contract was signed.

Another event has become part of our family folklore. Louise and I were invited to a gala dinner at Adidas headquarters in Germany to celebrate their 25th anniversary. I could not believe our luck when I looked at the table plan. There were tables of ten and the host of our particular table was Franz Beckenbauer, one of the greatest footballers of all time. Louise had been educated at a ballet school and had zero interest in football. I could not believe my ears when she peered across the table (it was pre-contact lens days) and said, 'Excuse me, Mr Beckenbauer, what do you do for a living?' The table went very quiet. His response was brilliant – he said he was a runner and would she like a trot around the dance floor. Louise said his footwork was immaculate.

Peter Black Toiletries & Cosmetics

The Americans have always been at the forefront of finding innovative approaches to product marketing. Having witnessed the growth of merchandise associated with Christmas and birthdays, they saw potential for the sale of gifts at Easter, Mother's Day, Father's Day and Halloween. We observed that one of the more popular gifts was toilet bags containing bath foam, shampoo, soap etc. This development prompted us in 1983 to buy a small toiletry manufacturer in Trowbridge near Bath, followed soon after by a cosmetics company. We then recruited the appropriate management and built the most modern production facilities. Our strategy was to concentrate on enhanced products through which we could demonstrate outstanding value when they were compared with the leading brands. By the early 1990s the sales of Peter Black Toiletries & Cosmetics were over £40 million (£80 million in today's money).

Peter Black Homeware

In the early 1970s, as opposed to selling individual items of clothing, the leading clothing retailers like Next and Benetton developed full outfits of jackets, trousers, shirts, ties and shoes which were style- and colour-coordinated. We noticed in the United States that homeware companies like Pennsylvania House and

Ethan & Allen were adopting the same strategy and offering their customers whole rooms of coordinated product. In partnership with Marks & Spencer, we resolved to be the first in Europe to follow this new 'dress the home' trend from the States. We developed our own lighting production facility and bought companies that made home textiles, hard and soft furniture and pottery (Hornsea Pottery). In addition we imported, through our offices in the Far East, ceramics and wicker furniture. This venture took longer than expected to get off the ground. In retrospect, I now realise that our expectations were unrealistic in that it took more time than we anticipated for the fashion for coordination to take hold.

Factory Shops & Retail Outlets

Everyone loves a bargain. Like many manufacturers, we were frustrated retailers. As regards generating adrenaline, there is little to rival the sight of money crossing the counter. In the 1970s, prior to the IT revolution, stock control and sales information were not as sophisticated as today. Consequently, there were more over-makes resulting in redundant merchandise. This reality, plus the problem of disposing of reject stock, was behind the emergence in the United States of individual factory shops and factory outlet villages. Yet again we took our lead from across the Atlantic. We were among the first to open a chain of factory shops (The Original

Factory Shop) and a retail outlet village (Hornsea Freeport). This new activity rapidly achieved scale.

Peter Black Distribution

The arrival of barcodes and EPOS (Electronic Point of Sale) in the mid-70s were early manifestations of the IT revolution. We recognised before most the substantial benefits that could be derived from positively embracing this new technology. More accurate and up-to-date sales information would enable us to respond faster to customer demand and reduce work in progress and stock. We therefore decided to set up Peter Black Distribution as a stand-alone centre of excellence to provide full logistic support to all the companies in the Peter Black group. By recruiting and training specialist management and investing in modern warehouse facilities, we effectively gave ourselves a competitive edge. A new profit centre for us emerged as it became clear that it was not viable for smaller companies to mirror the development of Peter Black Distribution. In order to interface with the increasingly sophisticated systems of the major retailers, a growing number of suppliers outsourced their warehousing and distribution to Peter Black Distribution. Peter Black Distribution's services covered freight forwarding, customs clearance, warehousing, pre-retail processing, label printing and transport. By 2007, we had over 1.5 million square feet of warehouse space and, as I said previously, an agreement with Marks & Spencer themselves to process 50 million units of clothing from Asia per week.

Peter Black Healthcare

In 1990 we bought English Grains, which produced vitamins and natural remedies. The reasons for this diversification were two-fold. First, we saw, in the United States, a growing interest in vitamins and natural products. Secondly, in common with our successful toiletries and cosmetics business, vitamins were low-priced consumables whose sales were relatively unaffected by downturns in the economy. English Grains had two established routes to market – brands (Red Kooga Ginseng, Natracalm and Calcia) which were sold through chemist shops, and Nature's Best, a well-established mail order business. We added Peter Black's speciality, which was private label supply to the leading supermarkets. The business flourished and we invested in a state-of-the-art new factory. In 2005 the sales of Peter Black Healthcare had reached over £40 million.

Exports

Coming from abroad, my father always had an international outlook. Exporting our products was a priority. In the early days, we had agents selling our bags and footwear throughout Europe and Canada. In 1972 Peter Black was awarded the OBE on account of our export sales. Thomas and I were fortunate to have a cosmopolitan upbringing in that we had many holidays in different countries and were encouraged to learn foreign languages. In the 1980s and 1990s Thomas negotiated know-how deals in South Africa, Canada, Australia, New Zealand, Yugoslavia and Indonesia, whereby local companies manufactured our products under licence.

1988 was a critical year for the business. There were clear signs that the economy was overheating. Interest rates were rising and Peter Black's turnover was growing at a faster rate than its profit. We decided to prune the tree in order to sustain further growth. No product category is entirely recession-proof but some are more recession-resistant than others. It became clear that sales of non-essential products fall off the cliff alarmingly when interest rates rise. Against this background, we started a process of selling the different companies in the Homeware Division. We did not consider factory shops and outlet villages to be a core activity and therefore they too were sold off. Having seen the recent success of Bicester Village, perhaps this was not one of our better decisions.

The success of the Adidas business was a double-edged sword. On the plus side, it was a fast-expanding and profitable business. On the minus side, it meant that a growing proportion of our total business was a brand that we did not own or control. This was the main reason behind the sale of Peter Black Leisurewear back to Adidas. We withdrew from activities which could not produce a satisfactory return in adverse economic conditions and did not have the potential for long-term growth. Our clear priority was to focus our management and financial resource on core/ essential everyday products and services – footwear and accessories, toiletries and cosmetics, vitamin and healthcare products, and logistics.

In 2000 we became concerned that our share price did not reflect the progress and value of the business. We had deliberately built a company with several divisions. In our opinion, being a 'table with several legs' yielded increased resilience and decreased volatility. However, for various reasons, conglomerates were now out of fashion. A conglomerate is the combination of two or more companies usually engaged in entirely different businesses that fall under one corporate group, usually involving a parent company and many subsidiaries. Often, a conglomerate is a multi-industry company. Conglomerates are often large and multinational. Conglomerates were popular in the 1960s due to a combination of low interest rates and a repeating bear/bull market, which allowed the conglomerates to buy companies in leveraged buyouts, sometimes at temporarily deflated values. Famous examples from the 1960s include Ling–Temco–Vought, ITT Corporation and Litton Industries.

For many years the factors mentioned above were enough to make the company's stock price rise, as companies were often valued largely on their return on investment. The aggressive nature of the conglomerators themselves was enough to make many investors, who saw a 'powerful' and seemingly unstoppable force in business, buy their stock. High stock prices allowed them to raise more loans, based on the value of their stock, and thereby buy even more companies. This led to a chain reaction, which allowed them to grow very rapidly.

The defining moment for us was when it was pointed out that a competitor of Peter Black Healthcare, whose performance was less impressive than ours, actually had a higher market capitalisation than the entire Peter Black group. It therefore followed that if the component parts of the Peter Black group stood alone, they would attract more value than the whole. Based on this observation, we decided to take the business private. This course of action also appealed to us for another reason. Thomas and I had long before decided that Peter Black would not be a traditional family business, and at some time in the future we would sell up. Taking the business private and then selling off the individual companies would be the route to an elegant exit for the Black family.

The 'take private' was completed in 2001. Peter Black Healthcare was sold to an American company in 2003. The remaining companies were sold to Li & Fung (an international trading company based in Hong Kong) in 2007.

Those seven years were the least enjoyable of my business career. It seemed to take an inordinate amount of time to get deals over the line. As opposed to being close to the product and the customer, which was my preference, I spent long hours in meetings with lawyers, accountants and bankers.

Since 2007, with my brother Thomas, I have been running Black Family Investments, which has a range of investments in the UK and abroad. In addition, I have had some interesting involvements from which I have continued to learn a great deal. The most high-profile was an investment in High Street TV, of which I was Non-Executive Chairman from January 2007 until June 2015. There will be more about this later.

Thomas and I both live in Ilkley. We enjoyed the 20-minute drive over the moors to our head office in Keighley. When we exited the business we moved our family office to a modern building, which also houses our car collection, near Skipton. I always enjoyed the solitude of the morning drive. It gave me time to marshal my thoughts and plan for the day. It probably was a bit dangerous in that I know the road so well that I was virtually on auto pilot. En route to the office, one goes through a small village called Silsden. It's a family joke regarding the number of times over the years that I have been fined for speeding going down the hill into Silsden. The final straw was three years ago at 6.45 in the morning – half way down the hill a policeman with a camera jumped out and waved me down. His opening comment was no surprise to me: 'I've been waiting for you, Mr Black'. To which I responded, 'I got here as quickly as I could'. Sadly, he did not appreciate my sense of humour and that meant another three penalty points on my driving licence.

CHAPTER TWO

THREE STAGES

Looking back, it is clear that Peter Black went through three distinct stages on its 60-year journey, starting in 1947 through to the final sell-off in 2007. I have observed that many other companies that have expanded over the years have had a similar pattern of growth.

Stage One

The first stage is the start-up period. The founder is often a dynamic and hard-working entrepreneur who runs the business 'off the seat of his pants'. The danger is that there is an absence of systems of control, and the business relies on the strength of personality and example of the owner.

Fortunately, my father was an enlightened founder. He recognised that if the business was to go to the next stage, things had to change. He encouraged Thomas and me to bring in additional young management and to broaden the product range. His approach was: get into trouble for the mistakes you make, rather than the ones you don't make. I remember going to a trade fair in Germany and seeing a range of shopping bags made out of a new polyurethane-based material called Vistram which looked and felt like soft leather. I found out the name of the German manufacturer and ordered 1,000 metres. When I got back to the office, with some trepidation I showed a cutting of the material to PB and told him about the speculative order I had placed. His reaction was not what I expected. He said, 'You idiot, you should have ordered 10,000 metres.'

PB jokingly said the business should be called Thomas and Gordon Black and Father Limited. Everything used to be much more formal. My father was Mr Black and Thomas and I were Mr Thomas and Mr Gordon. All this could be slightly confusing, and led to some amusing incidents. Thomas paid a visit to our Skipton factory. On arrival, he came face to face with a new cleaner who did not recognise him. In a forthright Yorkshire way, she asked, 'Who are you?' Thomas replied indignantly, 'Mr Thomas'. It was clear to Thomas that she did not realise who he was. He was quick off the mark and saw this as an opportunity to gain some intelligence. He said, 'I've come for a job, what's it like here?' The cleaner's response is now part of our history. She replied, 'Well, the money's good, you have to work hard, the old man is a real charmer, but his eldest son is a right b-----d!'

In the early days, we really lived the business. When I was at school and university, I received regular business updates from my father. Looking back, I have sympathy for my long-suffering mother. The family residence was five minutes from our head office in Keighley. Thomas and I both lived at home before we got married. Mostly the conversation was about business. The evening meal was early, at 6.30pm, so that we could go back to the factory and check the night shift. Saturday morning was mandatory – the only bending of protocol being that we wore a sports jacket and tie rather than a suit.

My father-in-law, Geoffrey Dawson, was a big influence on Thomas and me as regards the business and life in general. Geoffrey and my father got on well, although their approach to business was poles apart. My father was an energetic entrepreneur, hands-on, disciplined, and devoted to detail. Geoffrey was a more laid-back (I'm choosing my words carefully) strategist who concentrated on the bigger picture. It was Geoffrey who encouraged Thomas and me to take the business public. It was a measure of my father's open-mindedness and flexibility that he welcomed Geoffrey's input.

Stage Two

This is a critical stage, demanding a more formal and professional approach to structure and personnel. The objective is to reduce dependence on the founder's personalised style and put in place strong foundations which can support sustained growth.

As regards structure, pivotal to all the changes we made was the maxim 'small is beautiful'. Rather than one big sprawling entity, we put in place a decentralised, three-tier board structure:

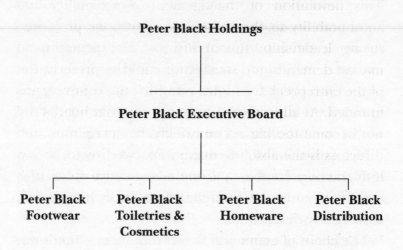

- Directors of Peter Black Holdings were the Joint Chairmen (Thomas and myself), the Group Chief Executive, the Group Financial Director and the Non-Executive Directors.

- The Executive Board was chaired by the Group Chief Executive and was made up of the Group Financial Director and the Managing Directors of the different operating companies in the Group.

- All the operating companies had their own board of directors, comprising the Managing Director, the Financial Director, the Production Director and the Sales Director.

This devolution of management responsibility and accountability to the individual operations promoted strong leadership, the ability to react promptly to market demands, job satisfaction and the preservation of the entrepreneurial spirit on which the company was founded. At all levels, it was important that boards did not become too big and unwieldy. In my opinion, ten directors is the absolute maximum. No director at any level was permitted to take on non-executive duties with other companies. We wanted them to focus 100 per cent without any distractions.

The chain of command was crystal clear – there was no hiding place for our managers at any level. Their areas of responsibility and accountability were clearly defined. The pressure to deliver budgets was passed down the line. In this context, the following incident comes immediately to mind. There was a knock on my office door and in came a footwear production manager. I could almost smell the negativity. With reference to a production problem, his opening line was 'You've got a problem, Mr Gordon'. I did not let him proceed. My instant reply was that I did not have a problem: HE had a problem – his job was to bring me solutions rather than pass the buck.

We realised correctly that the management team that was in place during Stage One would need changes and additions in order to navigate Stage Two successfully. Some of the original team could adapt to a more professional and structured world, others could not.

In Stage One our financial controls were somewhat haphazard. In Stage Two, especially as a plc, we needed accurate and up-to-date financial data. Stephen Lister joined us as Group Financial Director in 1988 and he led the team, putting in place the appropriate systems and controls. As our product range diversified into toiletries, cosmetics, healthcare etc. we needed to bring in new executives with the relevant specialist skills.

Stage Three

If the vital changes required in Stage Two had been successfully implemented, Stage Three should bring more stability, and the day-to-day running of the business should be less of a challenge. Typically, more macro issues emerged:

- The advantages and disadvantages of being a family business

- Whether or not to grow by acquisition

- What are the merits of Non-Executive Directors?

- Whether or not to sell, part-sell or float.

One cannot be definitive about whether it is right or wrong to remain a family business. Specific circumstances point towards which is the most viable route to take. In our case, I am sure Thomas and I made the right decision at an early stage not to remain a family business. Thomas has four boys, my sister Josefine, who lives in the USA, has four boys, Louise and I have one boy and two girls. Feed in husbands and wives, and the politics would have been disastrous. I also think it is fundamentally wrong to compel siblings to join a family business when, given freedom of choice, they would have much preferred to do something completely different. In extreme cases, this sort of pressure can cause serious unhappiness. In addition, we would never have attracted the high calibre of management which enabled the company to progress, if all the best jobs had gone to members of the family. I am reminded of the old-fashioned Yorkshire mill owner who introduced his son to one of his foremen as follows: 'Smith, this is my son Rupert who has come to start at the bottom for a few days'.

On the other hand, there are certainly examples of eminent private companies that have remained family businesses. They have stood the test of time and are progressing in a fast-changing world. There are two examples close to home for me. My daughter-in-law is a member of the Fenwick family – their stores have moved with the times and are as highly regarded as ever. One of my closest friends, Ian McAlpine, is Chairman of the builders Robert McAlpine – they have consistently out-performed the competition and have maintained their position at the forefront of their industry.

If I had my time over again, in the interests of discretion I would not call a company by my own family name. A company's name should be simple and internationally pronounceable. Some of the mistakes that have been made are amazing. Did you hear about the Italian genetic engineering company called Gene Italia?

Acquisitions are a big subject. Peter Black's expansion was indeed the result of organic growth and acquisitions. Some of our takeovers were more successful than others. Looking back on our experiences, I have some hard-won observations to pass on:

- Proceed with caution. With a little creative accounting a mediocre company can be made to look more attractive – the process of dressing up a business for market has been likened to putting lipstick on a pig. We often found that when we got under the skin of an acquisition, there were a few unpleasant surprises. The Americans have an appropriate saying – 'there is always more than one cockroach in the kitchen'.

- Analyse the reasoning of the seller. One of my father's more memorable sayings was: 'At the outset, you have the money and they have the experience – after the deal goes through, they have the money and you have the experience'.

- It is advisable to have a clear action plan regarding synergies/cost savings ready to implement as soon as possible after the deal is signed.

- The process of getting the deal over the line can be long and frustrating. I do respect and value the input of lawyers. However, left to their own devices they do tend to play 'egg timer ping-pong' with each other. The principals on both sides need to constantly drive the negotiations forward and not allow the lawyers and accountants to get bogged down in unnecessary detail. If the professionals on both sides meet face to face regularly and debate and agree the relevant points, time can be saved and the ritual of signing in the middle of the night can be avoided.

- If a deal involves a fund-raising initiative, my advice is to raise more than what is needed in the short term. The reason is that the negotiations invariably take up more senior management time than anticipated. This distraction is bad for the business.

In my opinion, acquisitions should be a supplement to, not a replacement for, organic growth. I am sceptical, maybe even cynical, about companies which grow only by acquisition. Although they will not readily admit it, their rationale is often financial rather than commercial in that they are effectively muddying the water to avoid unfavourable year-on-year comparisons of performance.

From the time we went public in 1972 until the final sell-off in 2007, we always had two non-executives on the board of Peter Black Holdings. I really do appreciate the contribution they made. I do not go along with the well-worn joke about non-executives: What's the difference between a non-executive and a shopping trolley? A shopping trolley has a mind of its own.

In order to get maximum benefit, one should appoint non-executives who tick the following boxes:

- They should come from a different business background in order to bring additional skills and experience to the party. In the later years we had a leading City man and a senior board director from a global pharmaceutical company.

- They must be able to articulate succinctly and have the intelligence and strength of personality to question and challenge in depth.

I have observed that many companies are small-minded and pay their non-executives the minimum they can get away with. We always remunerated our non-executives generously as we wanted to attract the best – 'pay peanuts and you get monkeys'. A few thousand pounds more or less was immaterial in the context of the business as a whole.

One of the following routes is normally taken to exit or part-exit a business:

- Trade sale

- IPO (beware of being intimidated by professional jargon. An IPO means Initial Public Offering – in my day it was called a flotation)

- A deal with a venture capitalist or private equity firm.

A trade sale is easily the most straightforward and quickest to transact. However, I am wary of earn-outs. There can be a serious conflict of interest as regards what is best for the company in the medium term and what profit has to be achieved in the short term to deliver the earn-out.

The decision whether or not to proceed with an IPO is not black or white. There are pros and cons. It is a different world running a plc. Before starting the process, it is advisable to be fully aware of what is involved and embrace the necessary changes positively. It sounds obvious, but one must take on board the fact that the new shareholders become part owners of the business and have a right to expect the appropriate level of communication. I cannot stress this point too strongly. Good communications prevent misunderstandings, and in the long term help sustain the share price and therefore the value of the business. To my amazement, I have observed that some large national companies do not get this message. They arrogantly view the City with suspicion, and interface grudgingly with their shareholders.

Our flotation in 1972 proved to be a good move for both the family and the business. In blunt Yorkshire terms, Thomas and I were working hard but we were not flushed with cash. The sale of the 40 per cent of the family's shareholding that was put on offer by Rothschilds did, however, enable us to start our married lives with increased security.

From a business point of view, a quoted share price gave us a currency we could use to fund organic growth and make strategic acquisitions. By being able to grant share options to senior executives, we were better placed to attract and retain top management. Through effective communications, we retained the trust and loyalty of our shareholders. The City does not forgive bad surprises – our approach was always to try to under-promise and over-deliver.

Cazenove were our stockbrokers. Although we were by no means their biggest client, their advice and assistance were first class. Our presentations to the institutions were well-prepared. However, it was still nerve-wracking, as a poor performance could adversely affect the share price. I remember a day in Edinburgh when Stephen Lister and I made four presentations in one day – by the time we got to the last one, I was not sure what we had said to whom.

When we became a plc, I had romantic notions of what our Annual General Meeting would be like. I imagined a big hall full of shareholders singing our praises. The reality could not have been more different. We hired a small room in a nondescript building in the City. The small gathering was made up of people who had to be there – brokers, lawyers etc. At our third AGM I was very excited to notice during our presentation a young man in a donkey jacket at the back of the room. I thought to myself, 'At last there is a shareholder taking an interest'. When the presentation was over, I bounded up to him and introduced myself. His response was a major disappointment: 'Don't speak to me mate, I came to clean the room and got caught!'

I have observed that many company owners are inflexible and illogical when it comes to diluting their shareholdings. In my opinion, this is misguided. It is better to have a smaller holding in a company that is growing fast and increasing in value, than 100 per cent of a company that is going nowhere. As a result of the occasional share sale and acquisitions, the family's holding came down to under 30 per cent. As long as our business was out-performing its competitors and making progress, there was no reason for me to feel insecure.

An IPO does bring a loss of personal privacy. We had a professional PR company to try to ensure that all our press announcements were accurate and concentrated on the business rather than personalities. It is not uncommon for the press to get things wrong. Often they amuse unintentionally. We had an opening ceremony for Peter Black Distribution's new warehouse. The local paper (not a brilliant publication, but it holds a lot of vinegar) reported as follows: 'A sudden gust of wind took all who were at the ceremony by surprise. Hats were blown off and copies of the Chairman's speech and other rubbish were scattered all over the place.'

I have to admit, on a purely personal level, I did find it irritating when I went to play golf on a Saturday morning – I could be halfway through my back swing on the first tee, when my opponent would ask: 'Why did your share price go down last week?'

The rise in prominence of venture capitalists (VCs) in recent years is one of the most significant changes in the business world. Today there are fewer IPOs and more VC deals. Regarding the Peter Black journey, VCs certainly played an important part in enabling us to reach our final destination in 2007.

As regards sales, part sales and Management Buy-Outs (MBOs), the VC proposition is compelling as it delivers most of the pluses of an IPO without the negatives – no time-consuming requirement to interface with the City; less exposure to the media and subsequent loss of privacy; and it is less complicated to transact. I have learnt that one should never underestimate the time it takes to complete a deal. It can be damaging to a business if the key management is distracted and taken away from the coal face for a long period of time. On the downside, a VC-controlled company will often find it more difficult to raise additional funds for large-scale organic growth and acquisitions than a public company. In addition, VCs often structure deals with debt rather than equity. In layman's language, this means that, rather than subscribing for shares, they put their investment in as a loan and thereby engineer a swift payback so long as the company makes a profit.

Our chosen venture capital partner when we took the business private in 2000 was 3i. This financial institution was originally called The Industrial and Commercial Financial Corporation, or ICFC as it became commonly known. Through circumstances somewhat beyond our control, for example, the downturn in the economy, and our major customer, Marks & Spencer, running into problems, we did not achieve the forecast level of profitability. This led to a secondary buyout led by Garry Wilson and Darren Forshaw, who were starting up Endless. Both 3i and Endless recognised the strength of the Peter Black management team and did not get over-involved with the daily running of the business. They had non-executive representation on the main board that provided useful guidance and advice. The sell-out to Li & Fung in 2007 generated an excellent profit for Endless and helped secure the base for their outstanding growth in recent years.

CHAPTER THREE

LEADERSHIP

The most important challenge for a leader in a growing company is to develop a culture of teamwork and passion. To achieve this objective Thomas's and my approach was a combination of style and substance.

As a business grows and changes, enlightened leaders appreciate that the art of management is the ability to change one's style of management.

I have learnt that control freaks are losers while delegators are winners. I openly confess that in the early days, the business was all-consuming for me. I needed a nudge from senior members of the family and non-executives to stop talking about delegating and JFDI, i.e. Just (Blank) Do It. Thomas and I had to become 'conductors of the orchestra' rather than the 'first violinists'. To my immodest surprise, I found that some of our senior managers could do parts of my job better than me. I became able to generate time to think about the strategy for the future rather than being consumed by every detail. Robert Louis Stevenson got it right: 'Judge each day not by the harvest you reap but by the seeds you plant'. But this evolution had a downside for me personally. I loved the product. I felt I was becoming more of a 'corporate wally' and a Personnel Director than an entrepreneur, as my time was largely spent on liaising with the City and making sure that we had the right management in the right places throughout the business.

Thomas and I did recognise our responsibilities in that we had the last word on strategy and investment decisions. We appreciated that the wellbeing of our team of employees and their families depended, to a large extent, on us making the right judgements. Fortunately neither of us was a worrier by nature. When evaluating a business proposition, there was one word we found especially helpful – CONSTRAINTS. If a course of action ticked all the boxes and seemed viable, we tried to identify the obstacles or constraints that would prevent a successful implementation. The answer usually was the cash requirement needed and the appropriate management availability.

In the 1970s and early 1980s our rate of growth was such that we were actually short of management. Rather than taking on older managers from outside who usually came with set ideas, we decided to recruit young trainees straight from school and university. We appreciated that the trainees of today would be the leaders of tomorrow. As a relatively small company, I am proud of how we trained these young lions. Our approach was a combination of in house and out of house. The trainees spent time in different parts of the business and were sent on the appropriate professional external training courses. Keighley was, in a way, like a Jesuit seminary in that when we made acquisitions or opened new factories in different parts of the country, the trainees/missionaries were despatched to impart the Peter Black culture. Today there are ex-Peter Black trainees working in companies all over the world, and many of them still keep in touch with me. Several have said to me that out of the spirit of camaraderie which abounded at Peter Black, life-long friendships have been forged.

In the Lord Sieff era, the main directors of Marks & Spencer all had PAs (Personal Assistants). Two main advantages flowed from this approach. First, the directors generated time by delegating to the PAs routine matters and the implementation of agreed decisions. Second, the PAs learnt a great deal by being close to the seat of power. Many of the Marks & Spencer PAs progressed to senior positions in the business and with other leading retailers. I had two PAs who were a great help to me and both went on to top-level jobs – Chris Wood became MD of Peter Black Toiletries and Cosmetics and Robin Horsell left Peter Black and has made a great success of his own business.

As part of the training programme for young executives, we devised and implemented the Godfather initiative. A few senior directors (Godfathers) were each allocated six trainees (Godchildren) with whom they met regularly and mentored. These sessions were lively and were certainly of benefit to the trainees. To be a business leader, one must be a competent presenter. The Godfather formula was a first-class way to develop these skills. I especially well remember one of my Godchildren. At the end of a session, I said to my Godchildren, 'When we next meet, I want you to tell me what you would do if I gave you half a million pounds'. I expected them to present ideas on the sort of business/projects they would invest the money in. The Godchild who presented first took me somewhat by surprise. His opening sentence was, 'Well, the first thing I would do is stuff this job!' He was lucky that I had a sense of humour on that day. He is currently a successful executive at High Street TV.

How often have you heard a high achiever say: 'You can do anything, if you want it enough.' Taken at face value, this statement is nonsensical. I am five foot six-and-a-half inches tall and no matter how hard I try, I cannot become a Harlem Globetrotter. However, it is not black or white. There are many goals that can be reached through intense effort. I just do not accept it when someone is described as being born lazy or untidy. A work ethic, tidiness, good organisation and punctuality are all disciplines which, with determination and effort, are within everyone's reach. This all might sound quite simplistic, but this sort of logic does resonate with management trainees.

Today emails rather than the spoken word or letters are increasingly the main medium of communication.

It is therefore important to teach trainees to write in a clear, short and sharp manner. Long, shapeless and rambling emails lack impact and are a turn-off.

The effective chairing of meetings is an essential component of good leadership:

- Avoid monopolising the air space (not easy for me!)

- Try to get the balance right between letting directors have their say but not allowing them to bang on

- Strive to summarise succinctly.

I found having 'away days' with senior management once or twice a year to be very constructive. Being offsite with no mobile phones allowed and in casual dress created an environment where thinking could be stretched and where new ideas could emerge. In my day, golf was always a great sport for building business relationships. Sharing the ups and downs of a round was certainly a bonding experience. Observing how your opponent or partner handles the pressure during a game can be revealing – I hope I have not been judged over the years by my putting. However, with the current anti-bribing regulations, corporate entertaining has become a bit of a minefield. The challenge is finding a way to take people out of their day-to-day business environment to allow relationships to develop on a personal level. Outside business, as a school governor and a board member of a charity, I have always found 'away days' to be most useful.

I do believe in the old-fashioned virtue of hard work and leading by example. Indira Gandhi said: 'There are two kinds of people – those who do the work and those who take credit. Try to be in the first group as there is less competition.' Our Head Office was in Keighley, which at its peak employed over 1,800 people. The main entrance for everyone was through a factory yard where Thomas's and my cars were parked. Our offices were next to the main door. The fact that on most mornings our cars were there and our office lights were on before the 7.30am start, I do think was noticed. Although in the early days we were the sole owners of the business, we were conscious not to abuse our privileged position. We avoided excess in terms of remuneration and holidays. When we were in residence, as opposed to being office-bound, we walked the factory floor at least once a day and checked on the night shift a few times a week.

It seemed natural to us to remain in touch with the interests and lives of our employees. In the early days we had a marvellous Yorkshire lady running the evening shift for sewing machinists at our Keighley factory. On one occasion, out of politeness, I enquired about her son, who I knew was her pride and joy. The dialogue went something like this:

Me: 'Hi Amy, how is your son?'

Amy: 'Very well, thank you Mr Gordon.'

Me: 'Is he married yet?'

Amy: 'Oh no!'

Me: 'Is he living in sin?'

Amy: 'No – he's living in London.'

We also had a telephone receptionist who was a bit too plain-speaking. An incoming caller asked to speak to the Finance Director – 'No, you can't, he's on the toilet' was the reply. Another caller asked to speak to our personnel manager, Mrs Renwick. Our receptionist's reply was again more accurate than necessary: 'You can't speak to Mrs Renwick, she's taken Mr Jones's teeth to the dentist.'

Crippling bureaucracy creeps up relentlessly on a business, like Japanese knotweed in a garden. This problem is usually more acute in a fast-growing company. Often, managers are too close to the day-to-day running of the business to spot the dangers. The Chief Executive should be able to play the role of 'Bureaucracy Buster' – he/she must question and challenge and ensure that systems of control are kept simple and effective.

It seems to be that there are a lot of similarities between the worlds of sport and business. A soccer team composed of highly talented individuals will often be beaten by a team of less gifted players who work for each other and play as a cohesive unit – like Leicester City. The hallmark of a top sportsman and business leader is consistency of performance even in the face of adverse conditions. The most successful businessmen and sportsmen also share a common characteristic. They never seem to be in a rush – it looks effortless, they have the ability to dictate the pace. If the Chief Executive always appears under pressure and hectic, the business is more likely to take some wrong turns. On the other hand, if the boss appears calm and under control in the face of adversity, the business will benefit accordingly.

As regards the relationship with our customers, we adopted what we call in football terms a 'man-to-man marking approach'. This was based on the belief that our sales executives would not be able to win the buyer's confidence and trust if he/she was also close to the buyer's senior manager. It followed that we tried to ensure that our senior executives had a rapport with their equivalent-level manager at our major customers.

The same repetitive routine day in, day out can cause boredom which often leads to mistakes and underperformance. Successful businessmen and football managers keep their teams on their toes by maintaining a constant process of challenge and variation.

I remember my father saying that he did not enjoy being employed at the start of his career. He said that he was determined, if he ever became the boss, to strive to create a happy and enlightened working environment. He was the master of small gestures which showed he had an almost family-type concern for the welfare of his employees. He remembered everyone's birthdays and we had Christmas parties, and get-togethers for our pensioners. Everyone in all our factories and offices was presented with a chicken at Christmas, a chocolate egg at Easter, and whenever it was very hot in summer, production was stopped and everyone was given an ice cream. I remember a one-off example of PB's caring approach. He spotted a sewing machinist leaving the factory who had worked overtime (this was in the days when most factory workers did not have a car). He knew that this person had missed her relevant bus connections, so he insisted on driving her home, which was 10 miles away.

In the 1950s and early 1960s very few factory workers had their own cars. Consequently, one of the big events of the year was the factory outing to Blackpool. Even before we came into the business, my father insisted that Thomas and I joined the party. Picture the scene – there were about 30 charabancs (that's what they called big coaches in those days) parked outside the Keighley factory. My father propelled Thomas into one and me into another. The journey was never without incident. I remember on one occasion a girl swallowed a whistle as we were going through Preston (this is not a euphemism). When we got to Blackpool, although we did not know any of the girls, my father gave us both £20 and said 'If you see any of our girls, take them on some rides in the amusement park'. In the early afternoon Thomas and I were walking along the front when two good-looking girls smiled at us. We gave them the afternoon of their lives! We took them on all the fairground attractions including the Big Dipper. At about 6.00pm Thomas said, 'Well girls, it is time we all had better get back to our coach'. There was a look of puzzlement on their faces. One of them, in a broad Yorkshire accent, said, 'What bus, lad? We're from Barnsley; we're here for a week's holiday!'

Our determination to emphasise the team rather than the individual permeated down to every aspect of the business. For instance, when there was a request from the media for an interview, I tried to make sure I started every sentence with 'we' rather than 'I'. I regularly turned down journalists who wanted to concentrate on the Black family rather than the business.

The Northern sense of humour was different and reflected the structure of the local society where in numerous small towns a few companies were the largest employers. Many years ago I went to an old-fashioned music hall evening at the King's Hall in Ilkley. One of the star attractions was a ventriloquist. I do not think you would find the following dialogue between a ventriloquist and his dummy in the South of England.

Ventriloquist: 'What does your Dad do?'
Dummy: 'He works at Peter Black.'
Ventriloquist: 'What does he do there?'
Dummy: 'He makes toilet paper and light bulbs.'
Ventriloquist: 'What do you mean?'
Dummy: 'Well, that's all he brings home.'

Wherever we had a factory, especially in Keighley, we appreciated our responsibility to the community. In Keighley, we were the largest employers and literally pumped millions of pounds in wages into the economy of the town. Coming from abroad and having been made so welcome, my father certainly put a lot back. Among his initiatives were the development of the children's library and the building of the bandstand in the local park – he loved brass bands.

I too have tried to participate in the local community. In this context, many years ago I accepted an invitation to speak about 'business life' to the thirteen-year-olds at a local school. After my short presentation, I asked if there were any questions. I will never forget what followed. The specific question from one of the young boys was, 'What happens if a company goes bust?' I thought he had brought up a good point and was half way through explaining the concept of limited liability when a little fellow at the back of the room put his hand up and said: 'I don't like to interrupt you Mr Black, but surely if the trend of the business is adverse, one can always transfer one's assets offshore?' In a state of complete shock I replied, 'Hang on a minute, what does your father do?' He smiled at me and said, 'He's a tax consultant in the Cayman Islands'.

A well-known local solicitor told me that he had recently presented degrees at a local girls' college. As he was handing the award to one of the female students, he casually asked her, 'What are you going to do when you leave college?' The reply to this innocent question took him somewhat by surprise. She said, 'Normally I go straight home'.

My involvement in the Arts Educational School in Tring (music, dance and theatre) was an example of my business experience being of benefit to a non-business institution. My wife Louise and my daughters, Laura and Sara, attended the school. In 1989 the school was in dire financial straits and I agreed to become a governor. My first governors' meeting was quite stormy. I asked a question and the chairman stopped me in mid-sentence and said:

'Mr Black, you have to appreciate that this is not a business.'

My response was spontaneous: 'It bl...dy well is a business and, if it doesn't stop losing money, it will disappear.'

I discovered to my amazement that less than 50 per cent of the fees were paid on time. Clearly there were a few cases of genuine problems but the majority of parents just did not bother to pay promptly as they were never chased up. I insisted that a communication was sent to all parents telling them that if they did not pay their fees by half term, their daughters would not be allowed back. Ron Busby, who had worked in the City, was a fellow governor and a kindred spirit. We introduced normal business disciplines of budgets, forecasts and cash flows.

When I retired as a governor in 1997 the finances were in good order and the school has continued to prosper.

In the 1970s and early 1980s, as our sales of UK manufactured footwear and bags increased rapidly, we found we could not recruit enough sewing machinists in Keighley. Our approach was to open sewing factories in nearby small country towns rather than big cities. By being a relatively 'big fish in a small pond' we were able to establish our identity and build a spirit of teamwork and loyalty.

Good communication with one's workforce created a spirit of togetherness and a positive outlook. Poor communication would result in uncertainty and suspicion. The challenge for us was all the greater as we operated from more than 30 different locations. In order to overcome this problem we stuck rigorously to the following:

- Every Friday I wrote a *PB News* which was put up on every noticeboard in every location on Monday morning.

- We published an extensive *PB Newsletter* twice a year.

- I spoke to all our employees in every location in batches of 20 at least twice a year.

I do believe it is a plus if the boss is somewhat outgoing by nature. It is usually a good move to react positively when someone makes contact and wants to meet up. You never know what common ground will emerge now or at a later date. Too many people are too reserved and sniffy about the word 'networking'. It might seem old-fashioned, but I have found that Christmas cards are a good method of keeping in touch with contacts one rarely sees, both in the UK and overseas.

It is sad to observe that progressive businesses often go off the boil when a successful leader steps down. It is the responsibility of the board to make the correct appointment. Sometimes it is a mistake to appoint a new chief executive who is as close as possible in personality to the departing one. Different market conditions and different stages of a company's evolution need different leaders with different skill sets. Through luck and hopefully some good management, in Dick Leivers and Stephen Lister we had the right chief executive in the right place at the right time. Dick met Thomas when they were both doing National Service. Following a spell with Marks & Spencer and Courtaulds, Dick joined Peter Black in 1968. In 1987 he was appointed Chief Executive. Dick's vision, gregarious personality and understanding of the product were just what was needed as the company grew. Stephen Lister was promoted from Finance Director to Chief Executive when Dick retired in 1998. They both got on well and respected each other's abilities. This relationship made for a smooth transition. Stephen's accounting background enabled him to play the leading role in the buy-back in

2000 and in all the transactions leading up to the sale to Li & Fung in 2007.

Trade unions in the 1970s and 1980s were more aggressive and powerful than today. They regularly tried to recruit new members in different parts of the Peter Black group. The fact that they were unsuccessful was down to the caring and inclusive culture we created. The unions could offer our employees nothing better than they already had. I would have found it most difficult to have to communicate with our employees through an outside third party.

As regards the business, my father had maintained a high standard of fairness and integrity which was an example for Thomas and me to follow. As our labour force did not join the unions, we felt it would be wrong for the company to join an employers' club like the CBI or IOD.

As I am certainly an inexperienced author, when I had completed the initial draft of this book, I did ask one or two experts to read it and give me their feedback. They all felt that I should articulate in more detail how I handled important meetings with business leaders, the outcome of which had the potential to advance or damage the business. The short answer is meticulous preparation – the devil is in the detail. I thought carefully about the macro points I wanted to put across. To avoid being taken by surprise, together with my management team I tried to anticipate the likely questions that could arise and be ready with the appropriate answers. I always avoided putting myself under pressure on the day. For instance, I made sure I got there with plenty of time to spare.

Everyone is nervous to some extent. In fact, a little adrenaline is a good thing. As regards memory retention, I use a technique I discovered at university – I read the salient points before going to sleep, then read them again first thing in the morning. When I feel apprehensive, I get some reassurance from the fact that the person I am meeting will usually also feel some pressure to make the right impression.

I had an experience which brought home to me the real meaning of the phrase 'dry up'. I was given the sad task a few years ago of delivering the eulogy at the funeral of a young friend of my children who had died in tragic circumstances. There were around 600 young people in attendance and the sense of sadness was palpable. I was well prepared and therefore felt relatively confident. Half way through my delivery, to my horror, my mouth went completely dry and I had real trouble getting my words out. Fortunately, the experienced vicar recognised the symptoms and a glass of water appeared like magic and the problem was overcome. The moral of the story is, always make sure you have a glass of water on hand when making a presentation or speech.

No amount of preparation can guarantee completely the course of a meeting. In this context I had an experience soon after I joined the business. We made carrycots and prams for Mothercare. The founder,

Chairman and Chief Executive of Mothercare was Selim Zilkha who was a most handsome and charismatic man. He was ahead of his time in so many respects. At their head office in Watford there were no individual offices. Mr Zilkha's desk was at the end of an enormous open plan floor. It was known that he was a tough negotiator and it was difficult for suppliers to get price increases. On this particular occasion, I was well prepared and tried a slightly different approach. After giving him chapter and verse on why we needed an increase in price I asked him, 'What would you do in my place Mr Zilkha?' To my complete surprise, he said, 'Let's try' – he came around to my side of the desk and I went around and sat in his chair. I was conscious that the whole office was watching what was going on. I seized the initiative and said, 'Mr Black, you are one of our best suppliers, I've been very tough on you in the past – you asked for a £2 increase, but I'm going to give you £3'. To his eternal credit Mr Zilkha replied, 'Thank you very much Mr Zilkha'. Then he picked up my briefcase and walked out. The whole office roared with laughter and applauded. Although I still did not get the price increase I was after, Mr Zilkha won and retained my greatest respect and admiration. When my father died Mr Zilkha, without officially being told, found out the date of my father's memorial service and travelled up from London to attend.

There was another Mothercare-related incident. I could not have been a doctor. I am not embarrassed to say that I am rather squeamish. The modern trend seems to be for fathers to be present at the actual birth of their children. In my case, there was no chance. The week after the safe arrival of our first child, Laura, I was invited to a Mothercare Sales Conference in London. Imagine my horror when, after a sumptuous lunch, Mr Zilkha announced that Mothercare had sponsored a new training film for the Royal College of Midwives and we were privileged to see the first viewing. Having avoided my own daughter's birth, I had to watch a film showing the most graphic detail. I just managed not to pass out.

I have always had an interest in politics. It is therefore impossible for me to talk about leadership without mentioning Mrs Thatcher again. I am a fan! I do not agree with everything she did, especially towards the end of her term in office. However, the balance sheet is definitely in credit. Regardless of one's political views, it is undeniable that she was a rarity in that she was a conviction rather than a consensus leader. In business and politics, leaders are often frightened of their own shadow. Mrs Thatcher was proactive not reactive, and demonstrated immense courage.

Over the years there have been many practical jokes. Some, Thomas and I have instigated, others we have been the victims of. A famous one followed a visit from Mrs Thatcher to our Keighley factory and an invitation for me to attend a reception in Downing Street. I received a letter on Downing Street notepaper which was signed by the Functions Co-ordinator. The substance of the letter was that Mrs Thatcher was very impressed by our products and she would like to show them to the guests at the reception I was invited to. The reception started at 6.30pm – could I come to Downing Street at 2.30pm to set up the display of our products? We all got very excited! I nearly walked down Downing Street like a travelling salesman, tapped on the door and said, 'I've come to set up a display of my products.' But when I boasted to a friend about this prestigious occasion – his response was, 'You have to be joking!' I then noticed that the letter was signed by Mr I.M.J. Oker! Ironically, a few years later Thomas and I were genuinely invited to Downing Street and we did present Mrs Thatcher with a Peter Black suitcase.

I am conscious that my views on leadership might come across in an over-emphatic and strident way. For this reason my last word on the subject is a quote from Groucho Marx: 'Only one man in a thousand is a leader of men – the other 999 prefer to follow a woman.'

CHAPTER FOUR

ARROGANCE

In planning this chapter I have narrowly missed scoring a classic own goal. Fortunately, the Oxford English Dictionary's definition of arrogance was brought to my attention – 'having or revealing an exaggerated sense of one's own importance or abilities.' In this context, one could say that my writing this book is arrogance personified. I therefore want to make it quite clear that as regards business, my definition of arrogance is very different from the dictionary one. Arrogant to me means: inflexible, complacent, small-minded, dogmatic, stubborn, self-satisfied, against change, being a poor listener, having a dislike of being challenged:

- I have found it very important to have a positive outlook and to try new ventures – it seems logical to me that one will never know if one does not try out new products and ideas. Over the years I have often been frustrated by the negative outlook of buyers. Sometimes they seem frightened of their own shadows. The best motto is, 'test and learn'.

- It is essential to have the awareness and intelligence to recognise mistakes and have the flexibility and courage to take corrective action.

Coming from a background where my parents lost everything when they left Germany, Thomas and I have never travelled hopefully and have always considered ourselves to be too insecure to be complacent. We got the message early on that there is such a thin line between success and failure. Success is a journey, not a destination. One cannot relax for a minute. This book would be considerably longer if I listed all our mistakes.

Peter Black's progress over the years is really a testament to our flexibility of approach and willingness and ability to reinvent ourselves. Products which are relevant today can quickly become dinosaurs tomorrow. As the market for shopping bags and slippers declined, we refocused our management and financial resource on a broad range of footwear, toiletries and cosmetics, vitamin and healthcare products.

It is probably a sign of my age, but the pace of change seems faster than ever. Here comes one of my favourite lines – 'The global economy is now a reality'. Against this background, many traditional profit streams are drying up, and new and exciting opportunities are emerging. The complacent Little Englander lives in a cocoon and stubbornly thinks he has a divine right to resist change. In reality, he is heading for the rocks. Over the years, I have heard quite often the following unrealistic and insular refrain along these lines from Yorkshire mill owners: 'My grandfather was a weaver; my father was a weaver; I am a weaver, we're not busy, isn't life unfair!'

As importing from Asia opened up in the late 1980s, it was unpleasant for us to face the fact that the manufacture in the UK of footwear and bags which had a high labour content was no longer viable. The uninformed looked upon us with disdain when it became apparent that some of our merchandise was imported. If we had obstinately tried swimming against the tide and continued manufacturing in the UK, we would probably have gone bust and all jobs would have been lost. What is not always appreciated is that an import business also generates jobs in the UK in terms of designers, administrators, marketeers and warehouse personnel.

As businesses grow, it is a difficult challenge for the founders to maintain a spirit of teamwork and openness. All too often, success goes to the head of the founder, who becomes a larger-than-life cult personality. An example of this was Robert Maxwell, whom I met years ago at a business dinner in London. I was actually seated at the same table. He was a big man physically and he can only be described as having a menacing presence. Clearly he fostered a dictatorial style of management, in which freedom of expression was stifled – 'Nothing grows in the shade of an oak tree'.

In this context, I was amused recently to hear the following comment about a well-known, self-centred, self-satisfied leader of industry – he fell in love with himself when he was eighteen and he has been faithful ever since.

I believe it is a sign of arrogance not to listen to advice. My father died when Thomas and I were relatively young and inexperienced. When I look back, I now appreciate how much guidance we received from the older generation. One of PB's closest business friends was Jack Cooper, a Canadian who had a substantial sports equipment company based in Toronto. He also marketed our Peter Black bags and luggage in Canada. Jack visited us a few times a year and we benefited greatly from his experience, wisdom, knowledge and perception. His sons, John and Donald, are good friends of Thomas and myself.

If a business has a repressive culture, the senior management is usually risk-averse, and it follows that commercial opportunities are missed. The most successful companies have an open outlook and can accommodate one or two mavericks in their management team who have the courage not to conform but to take risks. The story behind the launch of Peter Black Toiletries & Cosmetics illustrates this point. We found in Italy an attractive range of toiletries and presented them to Don Trangmar, a Director of Marks & Spencer. Marks & Spencer had never sold toiletries. If Don had taken the conventional route to get approval from the Board, it would have taken months. Instead, he had a friend who was the manager of a small Marks

& Spencer store in the West Country and arranged with him for the range of toiletries to be put on display. The toiletries sold out in three days and within a year Marks & Spencer had a new multi-million pound source of turnover and profit.

This launch of toiletries in Marks & Spencer is a testament to the truism 'it takes two to tango'. Product development was often the easy part. All too frequently, the challenge was getting the political and over-cautious buyer to agree to a trial. At a senior level, we devoted a lot of time to planning and implementing a strategy and tactics to overcome this problem. It was usually counter-productive to go over the head of the buyer and approach someone more senior. Buyers do not like to be dictated to by their bosses, and they can then become impossibly obstructive. Often the approach was to make the buyer a hero. If a product was a success, we would heap praise and credit on the buyer. Sometimes we reduced the buyer's risk by offering sale or return terms.

A symptom of being dogmatic and inflexible is implicit in the often-heard refrain 'competition is intensifying and margins are irretrievably under pressure'. The reality is that there is *always* room to improve operating efficiency. Many years ago, I remember complaining to a friend about the challenge of maintaining profitability. His response was: 'You don't know you're born! In my company, I supply the motor industry. Never mind price increases! My customers are looking for price reductions every year. Necessity is the mother of invention. Our survival is down to the fact that we relentlessly seek out ways of reducing cost and thereby maintaining profitability.'

There is a fundamental difference between debate and argument. Arrogant people argue. Team players debate. In our business, the senior directors had a meeting in my office early every Monday morning. I recall one occasion when the noise level was such that people walking past the door thought we were fighting. It was simply fully committed management having the confidence to articulate their views passionately and without constraint.

Human nature is such that one can justify to oneself dodging unpleasant tasks and decisions by claiming to be too busy. This can be dangerous, as having to take action under duress is certainly to be avoided. I try hard to challenge myself constantly and prioritise in order to avoid falling into this trap. It's easier said than done.

It is usually small-minded to bear a grudge. Often, offence is not intended and insignificant in the scheme of things. The following is not original but it is a truism: 'The first to apologise is always the bravest, the first to forgive is the strongest and the first to forget is the happiest'.

As I went to university, I have no problem in saying that a degree can breed arrogance. Some graduates believe that their destiny is to sit in big offices and make big decisions. The reality is that major decisions tend

The Schwarzschild family in the 1890s. Gordon's grandfather Robert is on the extreme right.

My parents, Hans and Else Schwarzschild, on honeymoon in Venice in 1933.

An early board meeting.

Gordon and Thomas Black and Father Limited.

Thomas and Gordon with Dick Leivers, the Managing Director of Peter Black. I can't remember why we were smiling. Perhaps we had just received a big order from Marks & Spencer.

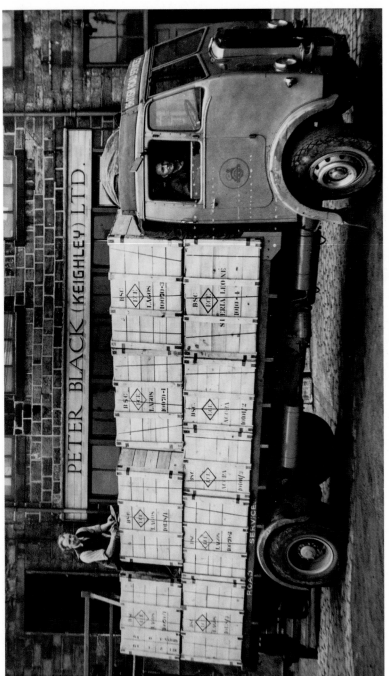

Crates full of bags bound for Lagos and Sierra Leone in 1952.

Peter Black directors pushing a Marks & Spencer van.

Thomas and Gordon presenting a Peter Black suitcase to Prime Minister Margaret Thatcher.

A copy of this Offer for Sale having attached thereto the documents specified below, has been delivered to the Registrar of Companies for registration. Application has been made to the Council of The Stock Exchange, London, for permission to deal in and for quotation for the whole of the issued share capital of Peter Black Holdings Limited ("The Company").

Peter Black Holdings Limited

(Incorporated under the Companies Acts 1948 to 1967)

SHARE CAPITAL

Authorised:		Issued:
£1,200,000	in 4,800,000 Ordinary Shares of 25p each	£1,000,000

N. M. Rothschild & Sons Limited

Offer for Sale 1,400,000 Ordinary Shares of 25p each at 105p per share

(Payable in full on application)

APPLICATION PROCEDURE

Applications must be made on the application forms provided and must be for a minimum of 200 shares and multiples of 100 shares thereafter. Applications from employees of the Company or its subsidiaries may be for multiples of 500 shares if made on the pink forms referred to below.

Applications must be sent to N. M. Rothschild & Sons Limited, New Issue Department, P.O. Box No. 185, New Court, St. Swithin's Lane, London EC4P 4DU, to arrive not later than 10 a.m. on 26th January, 1972. A separate cheque in favour of N. M. Rothschild & Sons Limited crossed "Not Negotiable" drawn in sterling on a bank or branch thereof in England, Scotland or Wales representing payment in full at the offer price must accompany each application.

No acknowledgement or receipt will be given. Applications received from employees of the Company or its subsidiaries, including executive Directors other than members of the Black family, if made on the pink forms provided. Acceptances in respect of these applications will not exceed 140,000 Ordinary Shares.

If any application is not accepted, or accepted for a smaller number of shares than that applied for, a sum equal to the application moneys or the surplus thereof will be returned to the applicant by cheque through the post at his own risk. All applications will be conditional upon the Council of

Copies of this Offer for Sale, incorporating application forms, may be obtained from the following:—

N. M. Rothschild & Sons Limited,
P.O. Box No. 185,
New Court,
St. Swithin's Lane, London EC4P 4DU.

N. M. Rothschild & Sons Limited,
4, Russell Street,
Leeds,
LS1 5TH.

N. M. Rothschild & Sons Limited,
Derby House,
12/18, Booth Street,
Manchester M2 4AP.

N. M. Rothschild & Sons (C.I.) Limited,
Hirzel Court,
St. Peter Port,
Guernsey.

The Stock Exchange, London, granting on or before 11th February, 1972, permission to deal in and quotation for the whole of the issued share capital of the Company. Sums equal to moneys paid in respect of applications will be returned by cheque if such permission and quotation are not granted by that date and, in the meantime, will be retained by N. M. Rothschild & Sons Limited in a separate account.

N. M. Rothschild & Sons Limited reserve the right to present all cheques for payment on receipt and to withhold letters of acceptance and/or remittances for surplus application moneys pending clearance of applicants' cheques. One condition of the application form accompanied by a cheque will constitute a warranty that the cheque will be honoured on first presentation and attention is drawn to the declaration in the application form to that effect. No applications will be considered which do not fulfil the conditions stated in the application form and the right is reserved to reject, or accept wholly or in part, any application.

Letters of acceptance will be renounceable up to and including 10th March, 1972 and the Ordinary Shares now offered for sale will be registered free of stamp duty in the names of the original applicants or the persons in whose favour letters of acceptance have been renounced provided that, in the case of renunciation, the letters of acceptance with the instructions contained therein) are lodged for registration on or before 10th March, 1972. Share certificates will be issued on 7th April, 1972.

The shares now offered for sale rank for all dividends hereafter declared on the Ordinary share capital of the Company.

Bankers

NATIONAL WESTMINSTER BANK LIMITED,
114, High Holborn, London, W.C.1.

To the Company: HERBERT OPPENHEIMER, NATHAN & VANDYK,
20, Copthall Avenue, London, E.C.2.

To the Offer: LINKLATERS & PAINES,
Barrington House, 59-67, Gresham Street, London, E.C.2.

National Westminster Bank Limited,
114, High Holborn, London WC1V 6LP
63, Boar Lane, Leeds, Yorkshire LS21 3SB
Beckett's Branch, 8, Park Row, Leeds LS1 0JS

Auditors and Reporting Accountants

PEAT, MARWICK, MITCHELL & CO., *Chartered Accountants,*
18, Cooke Street, Keighley, Yorkshire and 11, Ironmonger Lane, London, E.C.2.

Stockbrokers

CAZENOVE & CO., 12, Tokenhouse Yard, London, E.C.2 and The Stock Exchange, London

or the Company's Stockbrokers:—
Cazenove & Co.,
12, Tokenhouse Yard,
London EC2R 7AN.

Secretary and Registered Office

HELMUT ROTHENBERG, Ainedale Mill, Lawkholme Lane, Keighley, Yorkshire

Registrars and Transfer Office

BLICK ROTHENBERG & NOBLE, 7, Fitzroy Square, London W1P 6AS

Directors

PETER BLACK (*Chairman and Chief Executive*)
"Nordale", Green Road, Keighley, Yorkshire
THOMAS STEPHEN SHIELDS BLACK (*Joint Managing Director*),
"Longwood", Greenhead Drive, Keighley, Yorkshire
GORDON LESLIE BLACK, M.A., Cantab. (*Joint Managing Director*),
"Denwood Hill", 20, Hollingwood Rise, Ilkley, Yorkshire

HELMUT ROTHENBERG (*Secretary*),
49, Holne Chase, London, N.2

HISTORY AND BUSINESS

The Company was incorporated on 19th August, 1971, as a private company and has acquired from Mr. Peter Black and others the whole of the issued share capital of Peter Black (Keighley) Limited ("PB"). Peter Black (Keighley) Limited and Peter Black (Keighley) Limited. The Company and its subsidiaries are collectively referred to as "the Group".

STATUTORY AND GENERAL INFORMATION

£231,791 the Directors forecast that, subject to unforeseen circumstances, the Group profit before taxation for the year ending 30th April, 1972 will amount to not less than £525,000 equivalent after taxation to not less than 13.0p per share. The Directors intend to recommend a single dividend, in respect of the year to 30th April, 1972, of 12p per cent. payable in or about October, 1972.

(i) 19th January, 1972 between the persons named as section in (iv) above (1), the Directors of the Company (2), the Company (3) and Rothschilds (4), being the Offer for Sale Contract referred to above whereby the Directors agreed to sell and the Company agreed to sell to Rothschilds the whole of the issued share capital; in return Rothschilds had outstanding any bank overdraft or similar indebtedness, mortgages, charges hire purchase commitments, debentures or other loan capital guarantees or any other material contingent

GROUP INDEBTEDNESS

On 6th January, 1972 neither the Company nor any of its subsidiaries had outstanding any bank overdraft or similar indebtedness, mortgages, charges hire purchase commitments, debentures or other loan capital guarantees or any other material contingent liabilities.

(v) 4th September, 1970 between Express Dairy Company (London) Limited (1)

Part of the 1972 flotation document.

Gordon and Thomas with Princess Diana when she visited the PB head office in 1989.

Stephen Lister, Managing Director of Peter Black after Dick Leivers.

Founder and Chairman of Adidas, Horst Dassler (r), receives the Olympic Order from
IOC president Juan Antonio Samaranch (l) in 1984.

Jim Coleman and Andrew Malcher, joint MDs of High Street TV.

Gordon and his wife Louise.

Sara, Jono and Laura – Gordon and Louise's children.

to make themselves, and success is dependent on a disciplined devotion to mundane detail.

On business and social occasions, arrogance often rears its ugly head. We have all been to dinner parties where the person next to one talks incessantly about him/herself and never asks a question. Small people monopolise the talking, whereas big people monopolise the listening. I have heard it said of an arrogant acquaintance of mine: 'He is so up himself he spends his mornings in WH Smith signing copies of the Bible'.

Over the years I have met several leading politicians. Many are egocentric verging on arrogant. Even the most intelligent seem to be blind to the fact that a little humility could be a vote winner. It would resonate with me if a politician said something along these lines: 'I recognise that I have made an error of judgement, I have learnt from my mistake and it won't happen again.'

CHAPTER FIVE

PRODUCT

From the beginning, we were firmly committed to the belief that first-class product development was the essential catalyst for the business to retain its upward momentum. Put simply: 'You can have the most modern factories and the best systems, but without the right product, you're dead!' Thomas and I were not trained as accountants or lawyers. Fortunately, our first love was the product. Over the years we had a number of products which proved to be blockbuster game-changers – the corduroy slipper; shopping bags made out of soft polyurethane material as opposed to rigid PVC; Adidas bags; and more recently, at High Street TV – the Genie Bra, the XHose and the Nutribullet.

Looking back, I have made the following observations regarding the process of product development:

- Creativity flourishes best in businesses that have an open and team-spirit ethos, where conventional thinking can be challenged without inhibition.

- Innovation is essential – it is arrogant not to appreciate that when a shopper goes into a store, a switch in the brain clicks and a voice says 'what's new?'

- It is important to take on board changes in patterns of living and encourage customer feedback.

- It sounds obvious to say that one has finite financial and physical resource. It follows that effort must be focused on product which can achieve the maximum scale and profitability – the 'low hanging fruit'.

- Generally, we tried to focus on product areas where we had expertise.

- Successful product development is often the result of evolution rather than 100 per cent innovation. A good example is the Porsche 911 – the new ones are clearly an improved version of the old ones.

- The Impressionist painters did not copy each other, but they were influenced by each other. The same is true of the best product development. One should watch carefully what the opposition is up to. One should study product literature and visit trade shows at home and abroad.

- Challenge conventional thinking. When Marks & Spencer launched 'boneless chicken' someone famously said: 'Only Marks & Spencer could make a contract with the Almighty.'

- We observed that most of the new retail trends and products originated in the USA. We made regular visits across the Atlantic in search of new ideas.

In pursuit of developing winning product, we adopted a global approach which can be summarised as taking advantage of different centres of excellence. The boat shoes we made for Marks & Spencer were market leaders and represented a good illustration of the above point:

- The shoes were designed at our factory in Lucca, Italy.

- The leather came from a specialist tannery in Boston, USA.

- The sole unit came from Korea.

- The actual shoes were assembled in Thailand.

- The whole process was coordinated and controlled from Peter Black Footwear's office in Baker Street, London.

The shoe gene must be in our family. My son Jono is currently launching a revolutionary new shoe, branded Springuru, which delivers new levels of comfort as it has micro springs inlaid in the insole. The sequence of product development is a repeat of the boat shoe. The shoe has been designed and developed in the UK and the initial order has been manufactured in Vietnam.

'The sun always shines brightly on the other side of the street.' I have observed that often private label businesses crave a brand and vice versa. They are in fact two different worlds requiring different skill sets. For instance, if you have a business selling brands, you have to finance unsold stock to give a service, whereas a private label operation has less risk in that any stock holding should be the customer's commitment.

Effective brand management demands a high level of professionalism and specialist skills. You get what you pay for. Our experience is that one should travel first class and hire the best advertising and PR agencies.

We learnt that it is usually advisable to keep the brand tightly focused and avoid product proliferation. Hoover would not have become part of the English language if they had marketed a broad range of diverse products.

Brands require nurturing or they die. A good example is Yardley Cosmetics, which was a brand leader when

I was growing up. Today the younger generation have never heard of it. Peter Black's brand exposure was mainly at Peter Black Healthcare. Our leading brands were Red Kooga Ginseng, Natracalm, Natrasleep and Calcia. We decided to advertise Red Kooga Ginseng on television. Arrogantly, we thought we knew it all best. The first mistake was to penny-pinch in that we went to a second division agency which produced a commercial that clearly lacked impact. Secondly, we only committed to a couple of months' advertising. We quickly learnt that the whole exercise was money down the drain. We should not have started advertising if we did not have the commitment to continue in the medium/long term.

Another lesson was painfully learnt from our involvement with Arena Swimwear. Adidas launched the Arena brand and signed up Mark Spitz, who had recently won a basketful of medals at the 1972 Olympics, to front it. We were over the moon to get from Adidas the rights to the Arena brand in the UK. Almost immediately, we launched a comprehensive advertising and PR campaign. Looking back I can hardly believe the basic mistake we made. Our timing was all wrong – we created an appetite we could not feed in that the stock was not available until six months later.

The exclusive aura of brand names can uncover latent snobbery. We sold slippers to a Swiss retail chain where the buyer was pretentious to say the least. On one occasion, just for fun, we put a Pierre Le Noir label in a range of slippers. The buyer's reaction caused much merriment: 'I know Pierre Le Noir, I saw his latest collection in Paris.'

As I have said, our association with Adidas taught us so much. They appreciated that advertising was expensive and developed innovative ways of increasing brand awareness. The most amazing manifestation of the above was the Adidas bag, which was in effect a mobile poster. When players got injured during a big football match on TV, the trainer ran on to the pitch and was encouraged/induced first thing to make sure the Adidas name printed on the bag was precisely on camera. The Adidas bag became a cult product sought after by children and adults. Amazingly, the original Adidas bags with a Peter Black label inside are now a collector's item, frequently changing hands on eBay at around £100. Our attempts to meet demand taught us a fundamental economic lesson which, in retrospect, seems so obvious. At one stage we were manufacturing over 30,000 Adidas bags per week and we still could not supply promptly. Eventually the penny dropped – we were selling the bags too cheaply. We then slowly put up the prices until supply and demand fell into line.

Some of Adidas's product development was ingenious in terms of its simplicity. They were the first to appreciate what now seems clear to everyone. In a 90-minute game of football the players spend a fraction of the time kicking the ball compared with the time they spend running. This is the logic behind the fact that football boots now resemble running shoes rather than the big hobnailed boots that were around when I was young.

Make hay while the sun shines … a trick which is often missed! If one has a game-changing product which is clearly ahead of the competition in terms of concept and innovation, one has the rare chance to sell at a much higher price than normal for a period of time. We identified a number of such products over the years – the Adidas bag, the Organiser handbag etc. The extra profit generated made an important contribution to the growing value of the business.

Ironically, sales of certain products can be adversely affected by fixing the selling price too low. An example was a cosmetics range we developed for Marks & Spencer. Our range was inspired by, and not dissimilar to, a well-known, upmarket, expensive brand. Laboratory testing proved that our products performed as well as the brand. The brand had a specific product which retailed for over £20. Our equivalent product could have been sold at around £7 and would have returned an acceptable profit margin. However, this budget price would have destroyed the credibility of our product. It would have been seen as a turn-off for the consumer whose thought process would have been 'at this low price, the product obviously cannot perform as well as the brand equivalent'.

High Street TV had the best format I have ever come across for finding the optimum price at which to sell a new product:

- We launched a new product on a TV station at a specific price.

- We then monitored the sales very closely.

- If it sold well we edged the price up progressively until sales were adversely affected.

- In some instances when the initial level of sales was below our expectations, we lowered the price until the appropriate volume of sales materialised.

Over the years there were many occasions when we used targeted PR most effectively. One example was the launch of Hornsea Freeport, which was the UK's first outlet shopping centre. Expensive advertising was out of the question. We identified and briefed a PR agency which specialised in retail development/innovation. A well-worded press release was issued on the Wednesday; on the Sunday there was an article about Hornsea in the *Sunday Telegraph*; and on the following Monday, the opening of Hornsea was featured on the main ITV national news. The customers flocked to Hornsea and the business took off.

From the beginning my father was determined that our products would not necessarily be the cheapest but they would be the best value. A guiding principle for us was the conviction that price is only one component of value – quality and design are equally important. One must never underestimate the intelligence and perception of the consumer. Extensive advertising can prop up the sales of inferior products in the short term, but the truth will out. A highly advertised inferior product can be described as a weed masquerading as a flower. Marks & Spencer's large market share of various product sectors (they had over 40 per cent of the ladies' underwear market) was based on the consumer's trust in the integrity of the Marks & Spencer brand. Mr Gucci famously said, 'Quality is remembered long after price is forgotten'. We positively embraced Marks & Spencer's quality-control procedures, which were way ahead of their time. Prior to starting production, specifications were drawn up and were rigorously adhered to; all component parts were laboratory-tested and extensive wearer trials were monitored.

The success of a private label or branded product depends to a substantial extent on how it is displayed at the point of sale. Sadly, staff in busy shops often pay little attention to this point. We always claimed that if Marks & Spencer had displayed toiletries and cosmetics in all their stores across the country as well as they did in their Marble Arch store, total sales would have been boosted by at least 25 per cent. I could not help myself … I often found myself on autopilot tidying up displays in Marks & Spencer stores, much to the consternation of the staff. One of the reasons some major brands prefer to operate franchises in major stores is that they can then guarantee a high standard of presentation and service.

In China and other emerging markets, there is usually a strong demand for recognised international brands. The reason is that the growing number of middle-class consumers are relatively unsophisticated, and brands bring reassurance and status (China is now the biggest market for Mercedes and Louis Vuitton). Hong Kong's insatiable thirst for the most prestigious French wines is another example of the above.

In our experience, whenever we were involved in the purchase or sale of a company, the strengths and weaknesses of the new product pipeline were of critical importance in determining value. It was also seen as a plus if the company was involved in both private label and brand.

CHAPTER SIX

GOOD BUSINESS PRACTICE IS ENLIGHTENED SELF-INTEREST

I stated in my introduction that part of my motivation for putting pen to paper was my unhappiness with some aspects of current business conduct. This point is covered in this chapter.

When we were growing our business in the 1980s and 1990s, Marks & Spencer were one of the most respected and successful retailers in the world. They were our first and largest customer. They accounted over the years for 40–50 per cent of our sales. My belief that good business practice is enlightened self-interest is a most important component of my business philosophy. The simplest way for me to put across what I mean is as follows:

- I will explain some of the reasons for Marks & Spencer's success in the second half of the 20th century.

- I will then put the case and illustrate that the well-publicised problems facing many of the leading UK retailers today are due to the stark contrast between their values and approach and those of Marks & Spencer in the 'good old days'.

One of the main reasons Marks & Spencer were winners is that their products and their management team were consistently better than the competition. How come their product offer represented the best value? Put simplistically, the main reason was that they developed and maintained a long-term relationship with their key suppliers, based on mutual loyalty and integrity. Joe Hyman, whose company was a large supplier of clothing, famously described this seamless virtuous circle of trust as follows: 'Marks & Spencer are manufacturers without factories, and their suppliers are retailers without shops.' This environment gave their major suppliers the confidence to invest in state-of-the-art production facilities which enabled them to manufacture the best products on the market. A good example was Peter Black Toiletries and Cosmetics, in which we invested over £30 million in a five-year period.

Our relationship with Marks & Spencer was special from the beginning. In 1951, four years after my father started the business, there was a serious fire at our Keighley factory. Marks & Spencer immediately put a substantial sum of money into our bank account, securing our survival and speeding up the recovery. I will never forget the following incident, which might seem trivial, but meant a lot to me at the time. I had an appointment with the Marks & Spencer Chairman, Lord Sieff. When I walked into his office, he said, 'Gordon, you don't look well'. I said I was OK, but he persevered and I admitted I had a severe back pain. He said, 'Don't worry about the business today, let's deal with your back problem.' He picked up the phone and within 45 minutes I was in the consulting room of a top back specialist. John Timpson, who is a close friend of the Black family, recently wrote a book entitled *High Street Heroes*, published by Icon Books. His number one hero, not surprisingly, was Lord Sieff who also features in Icon's *50 Most Influential Britons of the Last 100 Years*.

Marcus Sieff reached the top of the group in the late 1960s and he insisted that M&S was an example of the best kind of free enterprise with a human face, something particularly relevant during the 1970s, which was a period of poor industrial relations with continuous strikes. He also fought against government interference and high taxation.

The *Guardian* obituary of Marcus Sieff included this appraisal of his management:

Five years after assuming the Chairmanship, and with a Labour government in office, he claimed that general living standards were falling. There were, he said, three reasons. Initiative was being stifled through taxation policies, there was conflict between management, and free enterprise was being progressively destroyed. He argued that employees must share in the success of a company, but that the taxman took much of whatever he gave to his employees. M&S was finding it harder to recruit good people. Many preferred to go into the 'feather-bedded' government service, where they had a secure life and inflation-proof pension, which no company that had to 'earn its keep' could afford.

In 1981 I was delighted to be invited by the senior directors of Marks & Spencer to a conference for their top ten suppliers at the prestigious Chewton Glen hotel in the New Forest. I was the youngest attendee and was keen to make a good impression. On the first morning, I was seated next to the company secretary. He was a charming man but did have two unusual characteristics – he smoked like a chimney and he had a tendency to fall asleep in meetings. It was my bad luck that these two traits kicked in at the same time. All of a sudden I could smell burning; I looked across and then down; my neighbour was fast asleep and his lit cigarette had dropped into my open briefcase. The rest of the attendees could not believe their eyes as I started pouring glasses of water into my briefcase. I did make it quite clear to all present that if I had not reacted quickly the whole board of Marks & Spencer could have perished.

Marks & Spencer's whole approach was devoid of arrogance. They regularly asked us what we thought they were doing wrong and what opportunities we thought they were missing. Of course there were disagreements, but neither side was petty-minded and we did not bear grudges but moved on. Friendships were formed which have stood the test of time.

In this context I recall an amusing incident. In the late 1980s and early 1990s, the director at Marks & Spencer we worked very closely with was Don Trangmar. Don was extremely able, most personable, but could, on occasion, be a little irascible. Sometimes he dug a hole which was difficult to get out of. I normally spoke to Don a few times a week. On this occasion, for some obscure reason, I was out of favour. For more than a week, he did not return my calls. I made an appointment to see him. To his secretary's dismay, I was still in her office waiting to be called in by Don half an hour after the agreed time. I had to come up with a way of overcoming this impasse. In Marks & Spencer's head office in Baker Street the corridors were patrolled by janitors in green jackets, wheeling trollies which were used to empty wastepaper baskets in the various offices at least twice a day. I had a risky brainwave. I persuaded a janitor to lend me his jacket and trolley. With my head down I knocked on Don's office door, behind which there were several people in a meeting around his desk, and I said in a mumbled voice, 'May I empty your bin, sir?' Half way between the door and the bin, they all recognised me and roared with laughter and applauded. Mission accomplished – normal service was resumed. Don was a great support to Peter Black. We still keep in touch and enjoy reminiscing about those exciting times.

Maybe it's a symptom of my age, but in these days of correctness and conformity, there do not seem to be so many characters around. One unforgettable character at Marks & Spencer was called Paul Bookbinder. He was not really cut out for the job. He survived on account of his legendary quick wit. Timekeeping was not his strong card. One morning, after 9.30, he found himself alone in a lift with Lord Sieff, who said, 'Late again Bookbinder?' Paul's response has gone down in history, 'Yes sir, so am I.'

It speaks volumes for the strength of the Marks & Spencer culture that the directors had got the message across regarding their values and standards of conduct, down the line to all employees in such a big company. This was made easier by the fact that Marks & Spencer were still, in a way, a family business, as the founding dynasties of Sieffs, Sachers and Susmans were still very involved. As with Peter Black, the family presence did noticeably bring an extra sense of care, long-termism and ownership. Most of Marks & Spencer's top management was home-grown and had come up through the ranks. I was consistently impressed by the high level of conscientiousness demonstrated by even the junior executives, who negotiated as if THEY actually owned the business.

Marks & Spencer were well ahead of the competition when it came to looking after the welfare of their staff. In the recession of the 1930s, the girls in stores were offered free hairdressing and chiropody. The rationale was that the better the girls looked and felt, the better job they would do and the more sales they would generate. Inspired by this example, we were one of the first companies to appoint our own factory doctor. When I trained with Marks & Spencer for six months after leaving university I noticed that their devotion to detail in everything they did was apparent to all. For instance, every noticeboard was immaculately tidy in that all announcements were displayed on the boards with a drawing pin in each corner. They had the same approach when they made regular visits to their suppliers. They famously inspected the toilets. According to their enlightened line of thinking, hygienic toilets means less illness means less absenteeism means a better quality product and prompt deliveries. When they went around our warehouses, they insisted on the tidy sealing of cartons and labels being stuck on straight.

When we started importing footwear and bags from Asia, our Marks & Spencer background gave us a competitive edge. By insisting that the factories we used introduced the quality control systems and human relations policies that Marks & Spencer imposed on us, we ensured that the products we developed were market leaders as far as quality and value were concerned. In addition, being a major Marks & Spencer supplier certainly helped our export sales – it was a first-class 'visiting card'. We explained the benefit of good working conditions. A high standard of lighting and hygiene would mean better quality products and less illness and absenteeism.

In all the businesses I have been involved with (including most recently High Street TV) I have advised the management teams that it is enlightened self-interest to treat their suppliers in the manner they would like their customers to treat them. As they say, 'You reap what you sow'.

It was a pleasant experience for us when we started sourcing from Asia as, for a change, we were the customer rather than the supplier. The hospitality and kindness extended to us was usually exemplary. We consciously tried to show our gratitude. A small gesture like taking them a book on Yorkshire or some small gift was always appreciated by our hosts.

Looking back, I now realise that Adidas shared a similar business philosophy to that of Marks & Spencer and this was one of the main reasons for their outstanding success. The Dassler family were active in the company and Horst Dassler was an inspirational and charismatic leader. Adidas executives lived the business and fought against Nike, Puma etc. as if their lives depended on it. Adidas products had integrity in that they, more often than not, both looked and performed better than those of their competitors.

One of the main reasons many of the large

UK retailers are struggling is that the balance of power between retailer and supplier has changed dramatically. In addition, the composition and ethos of their management teams have changed for the worse. There are of course exceptions, but many of the most prominent retailers have forgotten that loyalty and trust is a 'two-way street'. Their relationship with suppliers is like a 'state of war' or at least 'armed neutrality'. I will always have a strong feeling of injustice about the following experience. Peter Black Healthcare developed from scratch a private label range of vitamins and supplements for a leading supermarket. We went the extra mile for them in that we trained the staff and designed the point-of-sale material. The range was successfully launched. The thanks we got were that the customer internet-auctioned the contract for the entire range the following year! This type of short-term opportunism is the antithesis of the original Marks & Spencer approach.

Another example of the arrogant disdain with which some of the major retailers now treat their suppliers is the trick of arbitrarily changing the payment terms. In my opinion, this is tantamount to stealing. A recent report in the *Daily Mail* says it all. A retailer contacted suppliers announcing that it would be reducing the amounts it was prepared to pay, a further discount of 2 per cent from the agreed price. One supplier said: 'They screw you to get the lowest prices and then they screw you to get another 2 per cent. We have no choice but to stomach this. If we turn it down, we won't get orders next time.' With suppliers committed to produce these items, they are effectively taking a retrospective price cut. It is more difficult to name the major retailers who have not dictated similar unfair ultimatums to their suppliers than those who have. Some of the so-called icons of modern retailing are responsible for creating and perpetuating this demise of core values. This bullying behaviour is very short-sighted as suppliers will naturally take their best ideas to the customers for whom they have the most respect.

Another example of short-termism that now prevails is the fact that less management is home-grown. Many of the senior executives are recruited from their competitors. It would be an unfair exaggeration to call them 'hired mercenaries', but it is inevitable in these circumstances that self-interest increases at the expense of loyalty.

In the early 70s Idi Amin's brutal regime in Uganda intensified the persecution of the Asian minority, resulting in a mass exodus. For the Black family, this tragedy had special significance – it seemed very similar to Hitler's attack on the Jews in Germany in the 1930s. My father, Thomas and I felt strongly that we should be proactive. We decided to offer practical assistance to an Asian Ugandan family. The Lakhani family duly arrived in Keighley. We provided them with a house and we gave the head of the family, Harri, a job in our accounts department. Harri had been the manager of a big bank in Kampala and he was clearly over-qualified for his new task. In the early 1980s the family moved to London where they have built up a small retail business. We have kept in touch. Looking back, I suppose this is an example of a benevolent gesture bringing benefit to all concerned – Harri and his family got a good start in this country and we got an able and loyal addition to our management team.

Charlie Waller Memorial Trust (CWMT)

The Wallers are long-standing friends of my family. Louise and I were among the founding members of the CWMT and have devoted a lot of time over the years to the cause.

Charlie Waller was the oldest of three brothers. He came from a loving and supportive family. He was an outstanding young man – he built a successful career in advertising; he was very personable and popular; he was kind and considerate; he was good at sport and had a wide range of interests. Eighteen years ago, at the age of 29, out of the blue, Charlie took his own life. Obviously, everyone was devastated. Charlie's parents, Mark and Rachel, immediately set up the Trust.

The aims of the Trust are:

- Increasing public awareness of the nature, symptoms and dangers of depression

- Reducing the stigma attached to mental illness

- Encouraging those who may be depressed to seek help

- Alerting friends, families and employers to the risks posed by depression and helping them to identify the symptoms

- Training GPs/practice nurses and primary health care workers in successful methods of diagnosis and treatment.

The response has been amazing, which in a way demonstrates the size of the problem. We all know someone who has suffered or is suffering from depression or some form of mental illness. Although it is never enough, the Trust has achieved a great deal.

- We now have Waller Trainers in different parts of the country

- We are working in schools and universities

- We have an excellent website

- We have funded a chair at Reading University where the Waller professor is training psychologists and counsellors.

The basic fact is that if Charlie's family and friends had known then what they know now, this tragedy could probably have been avoided.

My reasons for including the CWMT in this book are two-fold. First, I try never to miss an opportunity to increase awareness and thereby help remove the stigma in the workplace regarding mental illness. Secondly, in a business context, I definitely think it is enlightened self-interest to be able to recognise in the workplace the early symptoms of stress and depression.

A joint initiative between Vitality Health and the *Daily Telegraph* reported that over 80 per cent of employees surveyed suffered from work-related stress. According to the Centre for Mental Health, stress costs UK employers £26 billion per year. This is why every organisation, regardless of size or sector, needs to take mental health seriously.

If an employee is suffering from an undiagnosed mental illness, the consequences can be very serious, both for the individual and the business.

It is a slippery slope from stress to depression. Even if the person is aware of the symptoms, there is often a reluctance to bring it into the open for fear of being labelled as someone who cannot handle pressure. This ignorance and stigma can lead to a dangerous downward spiral. Suicide is now recognised as the biggest cause of death for men under 35.

Great advances have been made in the treatment of mental illness as regards speed of recovery and preventing a recurrence. One often finds that people who have recovered from mental illness are stronger and more resilient in the face of work pressure, as they have learnt how to cope with it.

In a business, if someone is suddenly absent from the workplace, the other members of the management team are put under extra pressure. This situation is less of a problem if the sufferer is surrounded by colleagues who are understanding and the sufferer himself is not frightened to come forward. In addition, it can be damaging to a business if a key executive who is suffering from depression performs below par and makes mistakes.

Mental illness is a big subject. I do recommend that you have a look at the Charlie Waller Memorial Trust website – www.cwmt.org.uk.

CHAPTER SEVEN

TIMING

'Make use of time, let not advantage slip.'
William Shakespeare

'Time and tide wait for no man.'
Geoffrey Chaucer

'Nothing else in the world ... not all the armies ... is as powerful as an idea whose time has come.'
Victor Hugo

Any success in life and business is always partly down to luck and timing. There is so much that happens in life that can be classed as 'circumstances beyond our own control.' Sadly, we all know people who have had a bad roll of the dice in terms of illness and accidents. It follows that one does need a good slice of luck to be in the right place at the right time.

As regards my life in general, I consider myself to be very lucky. Unlike my parents and grandparents, there have been no major wars or times of serious hardship in my lifetime. I appreciate the following could be controversial, but I believe I was lucky career-wise to be around when Mrs Thatcher was in power.

At first her government seemed to be ineffective and Thatcher herself was restrained by the fact that the majority of her Cabinet were supporters of the previous leader, Edward Heath. She thought of them as 'wets'. Furthermore, a further sharp hike in the price of oil by OPEC led to a world recession and unemployment in the UK rose to the unprecedented figure of 3 million.

Her poll rating plummeted and was only rescued by her decision to send troops to win what became known as the Falklands War. Far from losing the 1983 election she won it with an increased majority. Now she could implement some of the policies she had longed to introduce. She could also remove from the Cabinet a number of the 'wets'.

Exchange controls were abolished, many of the nationalised industries were privatised, council homes were sold to their tenants, excessive tax rates for high earners were reduced and the so-called 'big bang' made the City more efficient. Her actions created an environment in which entrepreneurs could flourish. When she came to power, Peter Black had 600 employees; when she resigned twelve years later, we had over 4,000 employees.

In the world of business, to some extent you can make your own luck. A relevant definition of luck is 'when preparation meets opportunity'. Chance favours the prepared mind. Do not wait for your ship to come in – swim out to it. We were fortunate to be around when Marks & Spencer wanted to diversify from food and clothing into other product areas. However, our success was based on the fact that we DID recognise this opportunity and worked very hard to take full advantage of it. If we had put our heads in the sand and simply stuck with slippers and shopping bags, our business would rapidly have become a dinosaur. Poor judgement is regularly construed as bad luck. I have often complained that we were unlucky timing-wise when we took the business private in 2000. If we had completed the transaction six months earlier, the outcome for all would have been better. When I look back, I can see that I should have pushed harder for an earlier completion as the danger signs of delay were already becoming apparent.

I am amazed by how many senior executives suffer from what I call 'cocoon syndrome'. Typically, they have tunnel vision and say, 'We are not ready to sell for a few years.' What they completely fail to realise is that they do not live in a 'cocoon'. They must take into account the state of the economy and market when deciding on the optimum timing for an event.

Selling a business is inevitably a time of mixed emotions. On the one hand, there is a sense of relief that one has actually got the deal over the line. On the other hand one feels a sense of sadness as one is parting company with one's colleagues. For me it was very important that the business went to a good home. The sale to Li & Fung achieved this objective. Li & Fung are also a family business with a similar ethos to Peter Black. The team which had been supportive and loyal to me now had the opportunity to play on a bigger stage with a wider range of international career opportunities.

As I have pointed out previously, senior executives seem to change jobs more frequently than previously. I can think of quite a few well-known Chief Executives who have been masters of timing as far as their appointment and departure were concerned – some might call it jumping ship. The reality is that it is easier to make a bad business reasonable than a good business excellent.

Although new trends can be detected, it is difficult to predict the future with total accuracy. Therefore there is an element of luck in getting one's timing spot-on. When asked how he had made his fortune, Nathan Rothschild, one of history's most famous investors, said: 'I never invest at the bottom and I always sell too soon.' One should leave something in for the next man. It usually pays off in the long run to be generous rather than greedy.

If one is lucky enough to be in the right place at the right time, a hard-working approach enables one to maximise the opportunity. There are no short cuts. As ever, the Americans have some appropriate sayings:

- 'The only place success comes before work is in the dictionary.'

- 'Genius is 1 per cent inspiration, 99 per cent perspiration.'

- 'Only Robinson Crusoe got it done by Friday.'

Yet again, the worlds of sport and business have much in common. Gary Player, the famous South African golfer, said: 'The more I practise, the luckier I get.' (It has not worked for me. My putting is still highly suspect, but there again, I suppose I do not practise enough.)

I completely agree with these sentiments:

- 'Act in haste and repent at leisure.'

- 'Sleep on it – problems look different in the morning.'

When confronted with an important decision, some-times the most dynamic thing to do is nothing! Often, after thinking and discussing the issue at length, the clouds clear and the best course of action just emerges.

It is important to remain calm. I often think of the famous quote from Rudyard Kipling: 'If you can meet with Triumph and Disaster and treat those two impostors just the same; ... yours is the Earth and everything that's in it, and – which is more – you'll be a Man, my son!'

I believe that much of China's progress is based on the fact that their concept of time is different from ours

– they do not rush. Their recorded history goes back thousands of years further than ours in the West. Henry Kissinger allegedly asked Prime Minister Zhou Enlai what his thoughts were on the French Revolution. His reply was 'It's too early to say'. Stephen Lister and I had our first meeting with Li & Fung in Boston in 1995. We finally did the deal with them in 2007.

I have observed that as I have got older, I have become more cautious. Looking back, I can hardly believe some of the leaps into the unknown we made. To be more risk-averse is acceptable but one must not lose one's ability to think outside the box. I like the following, which is an example of creative sideways thinking in changing times:

An entrepreneur in South Africa was always keen on horse racing, and after the Second World War he bought a small saddlery business – at that time in South Africa there was a severe shortage of racing saddles. He was therefore amused to receive, in 1946, a letter from an English Saddlery manufacturer which read as follows: 'Regarding your order dated 3rd September 1939, it is now ready to be shipped – we regret the delay, but there has been a War in Europe.'

Now when these saddles arrived, a normal businessman would have sold them off at the highest possible price. But the entrepreneur had a different strategy – he went to the top three trainers and offered them each a saddle free of charge in return for two dead-cert tips for sure-fire winners. The result was that he won far more money than he would ever have got from merely selling the saddles.

I am not promoting gambling, but I am just trying to demonstrate the advantages of being able to think in an unorthodox manner.

The following is another example of seizing the moment in time. A friend of mine was a used car dealer. He was at the Huddersfield branch of a garage which was part of a big chain of garages in the North of England. He was offered 20 second-hand cars that had belonged to the reps of a large company. He bargained the price down and then said he had to make a phone call. After the phone call, he shook hands on the deal. It transpired that the phone call was to the Bradford branch of the garage group and they had unwittingly agreed to buy the cars from him!

I have described earlier how our business went through different stages. I am also conscious that the same is true regarding my own career. In the interest of happiness and wellbeing, it is important to get right the timing of changes in lifestyle. It would have been too extreme a change in lifestyle for me to go from the full-time Chairmanship of Peter Black (summer) to complete retirement (winter) overnight. My involvement with High Street TV and Black Family Investments softened the blow and enabled me to enjoy the autumn of my career. With the recent exit from High Street TV,

I have now happily moved from late autumn to early winter. Basically, I am still fascinated by the game of business. I do believe that my interface with the younger generation keeps my brain active, and hopefully I am helpful to them.

CHAPTER EIGHT

BALANCE

It seems to me that over the years pendulums more often than not over-swing. A particular event, trend or development can prompt a knee-jerk overreaction. The challenge is always to find the correct balance and middle ground before any damage can ensue. This reality is apparent in every aspect of life, including the world of business.

It is usually presumed that for a business to be a success, it must have the potential to achieve scale. However, this conviction comes with a health warning. 'Turnover is vanity, profit is sanity', or, in golf terms, 'You drive for show, you putt for dough'. Yet again, one must avoid the extremes and strive to achieve a balance. Out of choice, I would sacrifice some sales in order to deliver an enhanced margin.

Without doubt, the development which has had the most impact during my business career is the IT revolution. I was brought up with slide rules and carbon paper. When I first heard the word 'Xerox' I thought it was a Greek god. We thought telex and then fax were the cutting edge of technology.

I am concerned at the pace of change triggered by IT. The online world seems to be charging ahead almost out of control as to where it is taking us, regardless of the repercussions. For instance, will the impact of the rise of internet shopping and the demise of shopping centres cause the traffic in residential areas to be blocked with white vans delivering parcels? While there are, without doubt, so many benefits for business and the world of education, there are also real dangers to the welfare of society in terms of cyber-crime and the pressure and loss of privacy which social media puts on young people.

As regards business, IT developments are great time savers and the instant availability of data enables one to run businesses more efficiently. The downside is that, when information flowed more slowly, one could take one's time to consider fully important decisions. There is now no hiding place – it's an instant world. Failure to keep up can be very damaging. For example, in recent years Marks & Spencer were slow to develop their online business, which enabled John Lewis to accelerate into the space and establish a meaningful lead. If I was in charge today of a business like Peter Black, I would employ an 'IT geek' to make sure that we kept up-to-date and did not miss any new opportunities.

There are some worrying changes in the lifestyle and behaviour patterns of the younger generation. Many seem obsessed with their electronic devices, which render them antisocial and invade their privacy. It is sad to observe that texting teenagers are killing the art of letter writing.

It is progress at a price. We should strive to achieve a balance. The challenge is to embrace the new world and at the same time retain the best of the past.

I am amazed by how many intelligent senior citizens are Luddites and do not even own a mobile phone. Although they will not admit it, I suspect that the main reason they are burying their heads in the sand is that they are frightened of looking stupid in their attempts to master new skills.

I have experienced the dangers of the internet for someone with limited skills like myself. Some years ago, a friend of mine (we will call him Mr X) wanted to meet up with my son-in-law, Jim, who works in property in London. I laboriously single-finger tapped a note to Jim along the lines 'Mr X would like to meet you, a good guy – made some tin – rather smooth.' I then made a clumsy and catastrophic mistake. I sent the email to Mr X as well as to Jim. Mr X handled the situation with stylish aplomb. He emailed Jim and said, 'I would like to meet you, but I want to make one thing quite clear – I'm as smooth as Gordon is tall.'

Another business area where it is advisable to seek the right balance concerns the optimum level of debt. I must confess to being a bit suspicious when I see individuals who very rapidly seem to have acquired all the trappings of great wealth – 'all that glitters is not gold' is a truism. Those who are over-borrowed are the ones who can find themselves in big trouble when interest rates rise unexpectedly, as they did in the late 1980s. I have observed a trap which the newly wealthy often seem to fall into. They set themselves up with big houses, holiday homes, staff and expensive cars etc. What they fail to realise is the running costs of sustaining their new lifestyle. In my opinion there are no sets of circumstances which justify over-borrowing to the extent that one has to put one's own house up as a security against a loan. Nothing is worth putting one's family's welfare at risk.

Understandably, there is currently much cynicism about the reliability and support of the major banks – 'banks give you an umbrella when it's not raining …'. The state of a business should be a major factor in determining the appropriate level of gearing. If a company is ex-growth, it should be able to generate enough cash to avoid a high level of debt.

Alternatively, if a business which is in the right place at the right time can accelerate growth by borrowing that has to be the correct tactic. This was the approach we took at High Street TV (HSTV). The banks recognised that this was a business going places and were very accommodating. By taking on some debt, we avoided having to raise more money which in turn could have diluted our shareholding. This was important, as our intention was always to sell the business in the medium term.

Fixing the senior management's remuneration is

normally the responsibility of the Chief Executive. It is important to hit the right balance. Experience taught us that it is enlightened self-interest to err on the generous side. In a business like Peter Black which was growing consistently, it makes little difference in the scheme of things if the top team earn a few thousand pounds more. This approach enables one to be able to sleep at night as it reduces the risk of top management being poached by the competition.

In extreme cases, someone important leaves and the replacement is less capable and demands a higher level of pay than the predecessor.

The correct process of deciding on and justifying capital expenditure is a good illustration of balance and delegation. The decision to purchase expensive machinery should not be 'top down' – in other words, driven by the Chief Executive. Ideally, the initiative should come from the manager of the specific department. He should present the case for investment to his relevant director, who, if he thinks it has merit, should take the proposal to the board. Subsequently, the manager has the responsibility of ensuring that the machine delivers the promised efficiencies and cost savings.

There are so many aspects of a business where it is important to achieve the right balance:

- I mentioned previously the necessity for business leaders to delegate as the business grows. Again, the pendulum must not over-swing. The challenge is to delegate, but not lose control.

- When it comes to making important decisions, one must not dither and allow paralysis of analysis. On the other hand, it is dangerous to be impulsive.

- On the one hand, Chief Executives should listen to expert advice. On the other, they should challenge conventional thinking.

- When negotiating on prices one must not be a pushover. On the other hand, if one is too robust, the other side will 'add it on to take it off'.

- Publicity is a double-edged sword – too much is a turn-off – too little lacks impact.

If I took a snapshot of when I joined the business in 1965 and today, one of the most obvious changes is that management has become so much more technical and specialist. The days of the inspired amateur who read History at university are over. Nowadays, employers look for accountancy and law qualifications and MBAs etc. In this rarefied atmosphere of professionalism, I just hope there will still be room for natural instinctive 'market traders' who left school at sixteen and have acquired their skills in the University of Life. Ability and intelligence come in different forms. It is inadvisable to over-emphasise academic prowess. Some of the most intelligent people I know lack common sense. In fact, it should not be called common sense as it is not very common.

A consultant has been unkindly described as someone who asks you for a watch and then tells you the time. In my opinion, in the right circumstances, consultants' specialist knowledge and ability can be helpful. However, the brief given to them must be succinct and progress must be continuously and carefully monitored.

The challenge of finding the right balance between business and life outside the business is ever-present. One works to live – one does not live to work. Work is a means to an end, not an end in itself, and to be happy at home one must be happy at work and vice versa. I am wary of workaholics. They are often badly organised individuals, they run the risk of burnout and their narrow focus often renders them unimaginative and dull. It is sad to observe how many leading businessmen have broken marriages and unfulfilled private lives. Again, looking back, I now appreciate how enlightened my father was. Although he was passionate about the business, he always encouraged Thomas and me to take regular holidays and not miss important family occasions. This balanced approach has been an important component of our business philosophy.

Tom Lehrer, the famous American entertainer, said, 'Healthy mind, healthy body – take your pick'. Today this maxim has been reversed: 'healthy body, healthy mind'. The fact that businessmen are more health-conscious today is good news. The popularity of gyms, cycling and jogging is a clear manifestation of this trend. The success of Peter Black Healthcare, which manufactured vitamins, and High Street TV's fast-selling home fitness products showed that we did identify with and take full advantage of this desire to be leaner and meaner. Yet again, one must not go overboard. It seems to be that too many people have become obsessed with what they eat and how often they go to the gym. The answer is moderation in all things or, as they say in Yorkshire, 'a little bit of what you fancy does you good'.

My observation regarding over-swinging pendulums did, on one occasion, famously get me into a spot of bother. Lord Sieff and his top team paid a visit to our head office in Keighley. In the evening, we organised a dinner in a private room at the famous Box Tree restaurant in Ilkley. There were about fifteen of us around the table. Lord Sieff's gravitas and charisma were such that everyone listened to his words of wisdom rather than having a separate conversation. Boosted by an excessive intake of wine, I had the audacity to ask him: 'Tell me, do you believe that at some time in the future the pendulum will swing and the balance of power will be with the supplier rather than the customer? Perhaps the day will come when you phone me and say "I hear you're coming to London, I'll pick you up at King's Cross.'" There was a deathly silence, I thought 'What have I done?' To my enormous relief, Lord Sieff's characterful face cracked into a grin: 'Highly unlikely', he said, 'but I'll collect you at King's Cross.'

Another area where we constantly try to achieve the best balance is investments outside the business. Before the flotation in 1972, almost all the Black family's assets were in the company. This realistically meant that we had little personal wealth or liquidity. It was a case of 'water, water everywhere, but not a drop to drink'. Forty per cent of the family shareholding in Peter Black was released at the flotation, and over the years there were subsequent share sales and dilutions leading to the final sell-out in 2007. The challenge for the family has always been to invest wisely the money released from the business. Our approach reflects our background. Our inherent insecurity, caused by the loss of my parents' substantial wealth in Germany, is behind our determination always to have a good spread of investments. We aim to have our eggs in several baskets. In addition, our cosmopolitan background has led us to invest overseas as well as in the UK. A broad asset allocation does yield some protection against a downturn in any one sector. When making decisions on investments, it is illogical not to take into account one's reading of the state of the world. I believe the global economy is a reality. It is the Asian century and the United States is the last bastion of capitalism. Accordingly, our portfolio of investments reflects this view. It is important to draw the distinction between investment and speculation. For me, investment is a medium or long-term commitment. Speculation is inevitably a higher-risk game, but if one gets it right, the rewards can be substantial. Again, reflecting our background, most of our involvements are classed as investments rather than punts.

With reference to general wellbeing, a most important balance to get right involves the winding-down process as one gets older. It can be dangerous to one's health to work flat out and then completely retire overnight. I tried to line up meaningful part-time work, interests and hobbies to soften the shock to the system. I also appreciated that if I lost my mojo, the ageing process would accelerate. The brain is a muscle – if you do not use it, you lose it!

I am a great admirer of Warren Buffett. He understands the meaning of balance. As regards passing on assets to children, he famously said: 'You should leave your kids enough to do anything, but not enough to do nothing.' In this context I like the story of the old boy who got a new hearing aid. A friend asked him if he had told his family. His reply was, 'No, but I've changed my will three times.'

CHAPTER NINE

HIGH STREET TV

High Street TV (HSTV) has been the perfect swansong for me. It was fortunate for me in that both the business and I were in the right place at the right time.

I have explained that we regularly spent time in the United States with the objective of identifying and developing innovative products and new routes to market. The factory shops and outlet shopping centres are examples of American concepts we developed in the UK. Against this background, I needed little persuasion to get involved when I was introduced by Garry Wilson of Endless to Andrew Malcher and Jim Coleman in 2008, who had actually started and managed shopping channels in the States.

Here is a little background about television shopping:

Most of the people I know have never watched a TV shopping channel. Rather unkindly, although it's now changing, it was explained to me that historically the typical customer was someone whose favourite pastimes were watching TV and shopping. Initially I was amazed by the volume of sales a product shown on a TV channel could generate. The Genie Bra (a sports bra) for which HSTV had the rights in the UK, sold over 70 million units worldwide in 2013. One of the best-selling products of all time was the George Foreman Grill. There are two different types of shopping channel – those like QVC and Ideal which broadcast live from studios, and the likes of HSTV and JML which screen information commercials. Products which need explanation lend themselves best to this format.

HSTV is both an embodiment and an illustration of my business philosophy in that its defining characteristics encapsulate what I believe to be a winning formula. HSTV has made the challenge of summing up the salient points in this book easier in that I can simply explain how it ticks all the boxes I have alluded to in previous chapters.

- HSTV's initial route to market was obviously through a TV shopping channel. With the help of my connections, we started selling product to the major retailers. We then developed our website and also sold product off the page from advertisements in newspapers and magazines. HSTV became a genuine multichannel business, attacking the market on all fronts.

- The critical importance of consistently finding winning product was recognised. The development and nurturing of close relationships with the leading American DRTV (Direct Response TV) companies was therefore a priority. Such was our early success that we soon became the 'go-to' for American companies seeking to sell product in the UK. The three most successful products were the Nutribullet, the Genie Bra and the XHose.

- I have stressed the importance of achieving scale and margin. HSTV's growth was phenomenal. In its eighth year sales will exceed £70m per annum and it returns a very acceptable level of profitability.

- The directors initially focused the company's management and financial resource on the 'low hanging fruit'. In other words, they concentrated on areas of the business where high turnover and profit could most easily be achieved.

- They recognised the importance and cost effectiveness of PR. Several HSTV products were featured in national newspapers and magazines, and one (the Shakeweight) was actually demonstrated on primetime TV by Jonathan Ross.

- From the beginning, the foundations were laid to support a growing business in terms of management, facilities and systems of control.

- The management team was a blend of home-grown and expertise brought in. A few ex-Peter Black executives joined, including our former Finance Director.

- Andrew Malcher and Jim Coleman are inspirational leaders. Their different skill sets complement each other. Andrew was the founder of the business and is the upfront visionary and 'Evangelist'. Jim is the straight man running the business on a daily basis. They have created a can-do culture which reminds me of Peter Black in the early days. The component parts are a young, creative, energetic and enthusiastic team, bright and modern working conditions, effective methods of communication and, last but not least, a sense of fun abounds. I really enjoyed my visits to the office and usually came away reinvigorated.

- 'The global economy is a reality'. I have consistently emphasised the importance of having an international dimension. In more recent years, HSTV has developed its own product as opposed to just selling American products to which it had obtained the rights in the UK. We recognised that the DRTV industry provided the most innovative opportunity of taking a product global with scale and speed. We took our own products to the DRTV international show in Las Vegas and we then simply signed up HSTV-type companies operating in different parts of the world.

- As Non-Executive Chairman, my broad experience hopefully enabled me to bring to the business helpful input on several fronts. The other Non-Executive Director was my son, Jono, who had previously been a director at J. Walter Thompson, the leading advertising agency. His advice on brand architecture and positioning was most helpful. It was a great thrill for me to be working with my son. I never envisaged being in a board meeting with him, discussing the merits of a sports bra!

When the time came, all these 'ticked boxes' made the business 'oven-ready' for sale. As with Peter Black, I am sure that the takeover led by Endless was an elegant exit in that the business went to a good home and the team now have the opportunity to play on a bigger stage.

The HSTV journey is a textbook example of the advantages that can materialise following a VC's involvement in a dynamic business.

- In 2008 I was introduced to Andrew Malcher and Jim Coleman who were starting up a TV shopping business. Stage One began with me playing the role of a first stage amateur venture capitalist in that I raised the necessary funds from family and friends.

- When Endless bought out the initial investors in June 2015, it marked the beginning of Stage Two. High Street TV had grown rapidly and Endless, as a respected UK VC, could bring the firepower and professionalism necessary to realise the potential growth in the UK and overseas.

- Stage Three will be when Endless either sell to a large global VC or negotiate a trade sale or IPO.

For the Directors of High Street TV it is a win/win situation. The Endless deal provided them with the opportunity to take some money off the table by cashing in part of their shareholding. Under the new Endless regime, they will retain the shares which they rolled over plus, in all likelihood, performance incentives in the form of share options and bonuses. When the business proceeds to Stage 3, there is a strong possibility that they will be able to repeat the same process.

CHAPTER TEN

CONCLUSION

Writing this short book has been a good discipline for me in that it has brought into sharper focus my thinking on a number of subjects. Reading through what I have written, some of it seems rather strident or intense. As ever, there is a relevant quote from Groucho Marx which punctures latent pomposity. He sent a note to S.J. Perelman who had written his first novel: 'From the moment I picked your book up until I put it down I was convulsed with laughter. Some day I intend to read it.'

When I reflect on all that has happened, I can safely say that exiting businesses is more difficult and stressful than building them. When we were positioned in the right place at the right time, the business seemed to create its own growth momentum, whereas getting an exit deal over the line was a real rollercoaster experience. It is a dangerous generalisation, but in my experience selling businesses was more profitable than running them.

If I was asked what is the one most important lesson I have learnt, it would be how to avoid becoming 'busy fools'. There are always many business initiatives which appear to be attractive. The reality is that one only has a finite quantum of management and financial resource. It is essential to identify and focus one's firepower on the projects which have the most potential to generate the maximum profit and turnover (scale) for several years in the future.

'Shoemaker stick to your last'. A painful lesson I have learnt is that when Black Family Investments has invested outside our area of expertise, rarely has there been a happy ending. Too often, the business plan takes longer to implement than forecast. Additional funds are needed and if you do not subscribe, your original holding is diluted.

I always try to remember that the value and price are determined by the interaction of the forces of supply and demand. It follows that art and old cars can be good investments as the supply is finite and the demand usually grows over the years. Life is never simple. The downside of old cars is that the annual maintenance costs are substantial.

I am more convinced than ever that history does repeat itself. The study of history should therefore help us to avoid repeating the mistakes of the past. Confucius agrees: 'If one wants to define the future, one must study the past'. Against this background, I believe that the macro reasons for my Euroscepticism are compelling. Whenever in the past different nationalities with their own cultures and passions have been put together, it has always broken up acrimoniously – the USSR, Yugoslavia after Tito and Iraq after Saddam Hussein. I voted for the EEC (European Economic Community) not the EU (European Union). The letters have been changed without our permission.

I have another major concern which emanates from my conviction that there is a repeat pattern in history. My father lived in Germany in the 1920s when the government printed money (quantitative easing). As we have seen, hyperinflation ensued. Workers often needed a wheelbarrow to collect their wages. These conditions eventually resulted in Hitler coming to power in the early 1930s. There are already danger signs emerging. Extreme right wing parties are gaining ground in Greece and Austria and other troubled European countries.

In my opinion, a study of the past also demonstrates the inevitability of the rise and fall of civilisations. Detailed analysis reveals that there are similarities between current social and economic trends in Europe and those that prevailed during the decline of the Roman Empire.

The above is the rationale behind my belief that it is the Asian century. Nothing goes up in a straight line. The current problems in China are merely a hiccup. The graph shows an unstoppable upward trend. Ironically, one can argue that the main reasons for the Asian advance are, operating in reverse, the main causes of European decline:

- Asians live in a capitalist society which promotes and admires hard work, whereas in Europe, for various reasons, our work ethic seems to have declined.

- The family unit is strong in Asia. Within the family, the young look after the old and the affluent support the less well-off. In Europe, the progressive breakdown of family life and values is apparent for all to see. I partly blame the microwave! Mealtimes used to be the focal point of family life. Nowadays, more and more people snack throughout the day. No wonder obesity is a national problem.

- When I was young, it was regarded as almost sinful to be in debt. The unstoppable advance of the credit card in Europe has a lot to answer for. The idea of using one credit card to pay off the debt on another is anathema to Asians.

- The economic environment in Asia encourages entrepreneurs. In contrast, businessmen in Europe are increasingly constrained by a growing mountain of restrictive legislation.

I admire the tenacity with which Asians try to master the English language. I know I would find it virtually impossible to learn Mandarin! However, the language difference does cause some amusing misunderstandings. I have seen a sign in the window of a dry cleaner in Bangkok which said: 'Drop your trousers here for the best results'. On another occasion Thomas visited a shoe factory in South Korea where we were having some quality problems. The challenge for Thomas was to speak slowly in simple English to make his point. He started by saying, 'if we cannot get it right, let's go back to day one.' All the Koreans in the room looked horrified. He later learnt that Day One was the name of their biggest competitor down the road!

Another outcome of writing this book is that I am now an even greater admirer of the 'glass half full' ethos that prevails in the USA. I chose at university, as part of my History studies, to do a course on American History. At the age of 20, I made my first visit to the States and I crossed the Atlantic on a small Cunard liner which set sail from Liverpool. I will never forget my first sight of the Statue of Liberty and the Manhattan skyline as we cruised up the Hudson River. I imagined how daunting it must have been for those courageous immigrants who fled prejudice and hardship in Europe and arrived penniless, armed only with a determination to make a better life for themselves and their families in 'the land of the free and home of the brave'.

The success achieved by so many of the first and second generation citizens validates the belief that America is the land of opportunity. In contrast to the negative cynicism that is often evident in Europe,

Americans generally have a refreshing can-do, positive approach. I even believe them when they say 'Have a nice day!'

My father was, as ever, perceptive on this subject. He said that in a business in the States, if the boss had a new Cadillac, his employees would think: 'Great, the business must be doing well which means I've got job security'. In contrast, he said that in Europe, if the boss gets a new Bentley, often the workers' reaction would be: 'If he can afford this luxury, it means we are underpaid'. The most successful American industrialists, like Carnegie and Rockefeller, were great philanthropists. Their charitable disposition partly came from their strong religious faith. In addition, they were clever enough to realise that they had a vested interest in the perpetuation of the society which had enabled them to succeed.

One of my most memorable visits to New York was in 2011 with Andrew Malcher of High Street TV. Our mission was to meet up with the leading companies which developed product for the booming shopping channels. Many of the owners of these companies were either first or second generation citizens who had come originally from different parts of the world – Europe, Asia, South America. They were a personification of the 'American Dream'. The scale of the wealth they had accumulated in such a short period of time was mind-blowing.

The Americans love the English accent. The reason is that it is very upmarket to be of English descent. It is amazing to hear how many people claim to be related to the Pilgrim Fathers. The *Mayflower* must have been a very big boat when it set sail from Plymouth in 1620 bound for the New World.

New York is a jungle whose inhabitants come from all corners of the world and who are striving every day to make a living and get ahead. Their acerbic, sharp-shooting and impatient mode of expression is a reflection of their environment. Many years ago I was in the well-known department store Bloomingdales one Saturday morning. I came across a young man (probably a student) selling a hand-operated monkey puppet toy. As with a ventriloquist, the whole sales pitch came out of the monkey's mouth. It was all very amusing and I thought I would be a hit with my children over Christmas if I bought one. The dialogue went like this:

Me: 'I would like to buy a monkey.'
Monkey: 'Limey wants a monkey. They're in the box.'

I proceeded to pick a monkey out of the box. Having been trained by Marks & Spencer, I thought I had better do a quality check on my monkey before paying. To my surprise, the one I had selected had an arm missing.

Me: 'Excuse me; this monkey has a limb
          missing.'
Monkey: 'Man, they've gone cannibal. This is
          America – it's every monkey for
          himself!'

As I was getting the funds out of my pocket to pay (it was in the pre-credit card days), almost by way of making conversation, I said, 'What happens if I buy two monkeys?' – meaning, would I get a discount. The monkey's response was instant – 'If you buy two, you get a bigger bag!'

I love New York and, since that shopping experience, I have been a collector of New York humour.

- Influenced by the film *The Hangover*, a visitor stops a New Yorker on Fifth Avenue and asks for directions. The New Yorker keeps walking and replies, 'it's on the corner of get a map and f--- off street.'

- A gloomy New York businessman said 'Trade is so bad this month, the Mafia have laid off four judges.'

- I like the story of the New Yorker who came to work in London and thought Nat West was the name of a Jewish moneylender.

- On Wall Street they say an optimist is someone who irons five shirts on a Sunday.

- A laconic New Yorker said, 'Business is bad in the morning and slackens off in the afternoon – I'm not worried about the recession; I was a failure in the boom.'

I could go on ad infinitum …

So many of my contemporaries seem to be extremely negative. I receive numerous emails full of doom and gloom. It would be wrong if what I have written gives the impression that I am a pessimist about the future. I try to see every threat as an opportunity. My optimism is based on the IT revolution and the fact that the global economy is now a reality – therein lie opportunities in abundance.

The following is one such initiative which I would pursue if I was 53 not 73. The Peter Black/Li & Fung deal in 2007 was a pathfinder and blueprint for the future. Li & Fung, with offices throughout Asia, has unrivalled product sourcing capability. Peter Black has the product knowledge and customer contacts. The success of the Peter Black Division in Li & Fung since the takeover is proof that this combination of skill sets is a winner. It follows that there are many companies in Europe and Asia who would benefit from a similar deal. Against this background, I would set up a company called The Asian Bridge which would concentrate on making introductions and facilitating agreements between Asian and European companies.

I also now appreciate more than previously, that I have had fortunate timing and luck in abundance on my side. I had a job which suited my intellect and temperament. It was a passport to an interesting way of life. I have travelled the world and met fascinating people. In addition, I have also had fun. If I had not had a brother with whom to share the responsibilities and concerns, life at Peter Black would have been considerably more onerous and lonely. One of the few disagreements Thomas and I had was when my father died, regarding who should be Chairman. I said he should be Chairman as he was older – he said I should be Chairman as I led the interface with the City. The result was an unusual compromise – we agreed to be Joint Chairmen. Thomas insisted on being Chairman on odd days as he said he made more odd decisions than me. Thomas and I used to joke that we must not go anywhere together in the business as we might have had to make a decision! The serious point behind this jest was that saying 'I must discuss it with my brother' allowed us to buy extra time if we were not ready to take definitive action on important issues. I have observed that many successful companies are led by brothers or very close partners. At High Street TV, Andrew Malcher and Jim Coleman work as closely together as Thomas and I did with Dick Leivers and Stephen Lister.

As mentioned, I do believe in the importance of the sense of family in both business and life in general. For Thomas, my sister Josefine, and me it is heart-warming to observe the close relationships between all the cousins in the UK and USA. Every two years we get together for a few days of golf, alternating between the United States and somewhere in Europe – what goes on tour stays on tour.

We spend more time at work than anywhere else in a business career. The objective therefore must be, despite the ups and downs, to do one's best to enjoy it. I would be exaggerating if I said I got out of bed every morning and said 'yippee – I'm going to work'. However, on balance, I've enjoyed my working life and one of the main reasons is that there have been many amusing happenings over the years. I would go as far as to say that humour is an essential component of a winning business culture.

There were many practical jokes over the years. The ground rule was that the pain and concern must be 'short' and the humour 'long'. This is an important point as one does not want to cause undue distress. A good example of the above is the following. Thomas and some colleagues gave a dinner at the Box Tree restaurant for the head man of the British Shoe Corporation, one of our largest footwear customers. I knew the head waiter well and he was a willing accomplice. The restaurant was quite theatrical in that the main course arrived with a serving dome covering the plates, which the waiters then removed in unison. Thomas was surprised when his dome was removed to find a slipper on his plate. We also arranged for £500 to be added to the wine bill. Thomas apparently went white – he quickly recovered and started planning his revenge …

I am intrigued by some of the new jargon – much of it seems to me to be verbose and an attempt to mislead.

- When I was young, head hunters were a dangerous tribe in Africa.

- Printing money has become quantitative easing.

- Third World is now called emerging markets.

- When a company is said to have had a buoyant year it usually means that it has just managed to keep afloat.

- Critical shipments usually means late deliveries.

- Under-planned usually means that the budget has been missed by a mile.

- Thomas went with Alastair Henderson (a director of our footwear business) to a meeting at Scholl for whom we were developing a range of footwear. Everything went well until one of Scholl's team said, 'I presume you have A74B27 system of quality control?' Alastair looked shell-shocked. Thomas's response saved the day. 'We have Mavis and if she's good enough for Marks & Spencer, she'll be good enough for you.'

- In the old days it was easier to hire and fire. The modern way of dismissing an employee is to call them in to your office, sit them down and say, 'I don't know how we'll manage without you, but we're going to give it a try'. A friend of

> mine said he was being retired on health
> grounds – his boss was sick of him.

I mentioned the IT revolution. Did you hear about the micro technology company? Business was so good they had to move to smaller premises.

Following the sale of the business to Li & Fung in 2007 I have occasionally been asked to make after-dinner speeches. I had an opening line which usually got a good laugh … 'When I retired from Peter Black I gave myself some ground rules regarding future involvements. Having been "beaten up" by major retailers for much of my career, I said I would only get involved in businesses which had a good margin and worked with people I liked. You will not be surprised to hear I'm not very busy …'

I recently read somewhere the rather cynical view of the life cycle of a major product:

- Wild enthusiasm
- Total confusion
- Search for the guilty
- Punishment of the innocent
- Promotion of the non-participants

Some tongue-in-cheek advice:

- When in charge – ponder
- When in trouble – delegate
- When in doubt – mumble

Business is all about paying attention to the five Ps –
People, Philosophy, Product, Premises and Price.

Finally, my formula for success is:

Winning Product

+

Flexibility of Approach

+

Effective Leadership

+

Enlightened Integrity-Based Business Ethos

+

Good Luck and timing

= ✓

You can fight old age, but you cannot beat it! There
is nothing like the innocent remarks of children
for giving one a dose of reality. I mentioned to my
grandson, William, that I liked the study of history. His
response was, 'It's easy for you, you were around when
it happened.'

I cannot claim to have always practised what I have
preached! My hope is that what I have written will be
interesting and helpful to those who are now involved
in a fast-changing business world.

I was very fond of my late father-in-law, Geoffrey
Dawson. He had a fund of wise sayings. The one that
has had the most meaning to me over the years is: 'To
whom much has been given much is expected.' I have

had no real religious upbringing but, hopefully, I have a conscience and I appreciate that in life I have had a good roll of the dice. Therein lies my motivation to put something back and to behave correctly. I have certainly under-achieved in this department, but I will keep trying ...

INDEX

3i 55

acquisitions 48–9
Adidas 29–31, 36–7, 86, 87–8, 99
advertising 86–7, 90
after-dinner speeches 142
Airways 25–6
Amin, Idi 101
Arena Swimwear 86
argument, debate versus 80
arrogance 75–81, 96
Arts Educational School 67–8
Asia, sourcing from 98–9
The Asian Bridge 138
Asian century 122, 132–4
Avon Cosmetics 27
'away days' 60–1

balance 114–23
Bata Organization 18
Beckenbauer, Franz 31

Bicester Village 36

'big bang' 107

Black, Adam 19

Black, Ben 19

Black, Daniel 19

Black, Else (née Kohlmann) 14, 16, 17–18

Black, Gordon

  back problem incident 94

  Blackpool 64–5

  car collection 39

  early days in business 42–3

  early life 17, 20, 134

  family 47, 139

  impetuous nature 143

  retirement 112, 123

  speeding fines 39–40

  Thomas and 138–9

Black, Jono 85, 128

Black, Josefine 8, 47, 139

Black, Laura 67, 73

Black, Louise (née Dawson) 31, 67, 102

  family 47

Black, Oliver 19

Black, Peter (Hans Schwarzschild)

  balanced approach 120

  business approach 41–3

  car collection 20–1

  death 21, 78

  in Germany 14

ill health 21
move to England 16–17
OBE 36
Thomas on 17–18
on USA 135
Black, Sara 67
Black, Sue (née Broughton) 19
Black, Thomas
  and Black Family Investments 39
  Blackpool 64–5
  and cleaner 42
  early days in business 42–3
  early life 8, 17, 19
  Gordon and 138–9
  impetuous nature 143
  know-how deals 36
  marriage and family 19, 47, 139
  Scholl incident 141
  in South Korea 134
Black Family Investments 39, 112, 131
Blackpool 64–5
Bloomingdales 136
bluntness 9
boat shoes 84
Bookbinder, Paul 97
Boots 18, 23
Box Tree restaurant 121–2, 140
brand management 85–7, 91
briefcase incident 95

British Shoe Corporation 23, 140
Buffett, Warren 123
'buoyant year' 141
bureaucracy 62
Busby, Ron 67
business, sport and 62–3
business practice 92–105
busyness 80
buyers 79

Calcia 86
capital expenditure 118
car dealer incident 112
Cazenove 22, 52
chairing of meetings 60
change
    pace of 76
    timing of 112
Charlie Waller Memorial Trust (CWMT) 102–5
Chaucer, Geoffrey 106
Chewton Glen hotel 95
China 91, 110–11, 132
civilisations, rise and fall 132
'cocoon syndrome' 108
Coleman, Jim 124, 127, 129, 139
communication 68
community responsibility 66
Confucius 131
conglomerates 37–8

constraints 57
consultants 120
Cooper, Donald 78
Cooper, Jack 78
Cooper, John 78
corduroy 19
corporate entertaining 60
creative thinking 111–12
creativity 82
critical shipments 141
customers, relationship with 63

Dassler, Adi 29, 31
Dassler, Horst 30, 99
Dassler, Mrs 29–30, 31
Dassler, Rudolph 29
Dawson, Geoffrey 43, 143
Day One 134
debate, argument versus 80
debt
   level of 116–17
   personal 133
delegation 56, 118–19
demand, supply and 131
depression 102–5
Dick & Goldschmidt 14
Direct Response TV (DRTV) 126, 127–8
dismissal 141–2
Downing Street 73–4

'dry up' 71

earn-outs 51
emails 59–60
emerging markets 141
Endless 55, 124, 128, 129
English Grains 35
Euroscepticism 131–2
evolution 83
exchange controls 107

factory outing 64–5
factory shops 33–4, 36
Falklands War 107
family businesses 46–8
family life 133
Fenwick 47
five Ps 143
Forshaw, Darren 55

Gandhi, Indira 61
Genie Bra 125, 126
George Foreman Grill 125
Germany 14–16
'glass half full' ethos 134
global economy 76, 122, 127, 138
Godfather initiative 58–9
golf 60, 110, 139
Göttingen, University of 16

grudges 80, 96
Gucci, Mr 90

head hunters 140
Heath, Edward 107
Henderson, Alastair 141
High Street TV (HSTV) 124–9
    Blacks as non-executive directors 39, 128
    borrowing 117
    executives at 59, 127
    growth 126
    home fitness products 121
    investment in 39
    pricing strategy 88–9
    products 124, 125–6
    sale 128–9
    treatment of suppliers 99
history, as repeating itself 131–2
Hitler, Adolf 14–15, 101, 132
Hong Kong 91
Hoover 85
Hornsea Freeport 34, 89
Hornsea Pottery 33
Horsell, Robin 58
Hugo, Victor 106
humility 81
humour, as business culture component 140
Hussein, Saddam 132
Hyman, Joe 93

hyperinflation 15, 132

Ilkley 39, 121
    King's Hall 65
import businesses 77
inflation 11, 12–13, 15
Initial Public Offerings (IPOs) 51–4
innovation 83
investments 122–3, 131
Iraq 132
IT revolution 114–15, 138, 142

J. Walter Thompson 128
jargon 140–2
Jews, persecution of 14–16
John Lewis 115

Keighley
    community involvement 66
    factory 17–18, 61, 93
Kipling, Rudyard 110
Kissinger, Henry 111

Lakhani, Harri 101–2
Las Vegas 128
leadership 56–74
Lehrer, Tom 121
Leivers, Dick 69, 139
Li & Fung 38, 55, 70, 109, 111, 138

Lister, Stephen 46, 52, 69–70, 111, 139
Louis Vuitton 91
'low hanging fruit' 83, 126
Lucca 84
luck 107–8, 109, 138

Malcher, Andrew 124, 127, 129, 135, 139
Management Buy-Outs (MBOs) 54
Marks & Spencer
   boat shoes 84
   'boneless chicken' 84
   business practice 92–100
   buy British philosophy 24–5
   cosmetics 88
   as customer in 2000s 35
   displays 90
   as early customer 18–19, 23, 24–6, 108
   Gordon at 20
   market share 90
   'non-clothing' 28
   online business 115
   PAs 58
   problems 55
   relationship with 93–4, 98–9
   staff welfare 98
   Thomas at 19–20
   toiletries 78–9
Marx, Groucho 74, 120
Maxwell, Robert 77

McAlpine, Ian 47
meetings, handling 70–2
memory retention 71
mental illness 102–5
Mercedes 91
monetary values 11–13
monkey puppet incident 136–7
Mothercare 27, 71–3

Natracalm 86
Natrasleep 86
Nature's Best 35
Nazi Party 14–16
networking 69
New York 135, 136–7
non-executive directors 50
Northern humour 65
Nuremberg Laws 16
Nutribullet blender 7–8, 126

OPEC 107
organic growth 48, 49
outlet villages 34, 36

PAs (Personal Assistants) 58
payment terms 100–1
PB News 68
PB Newsletter 68

Perelman, S.J. 130
Peter Black
  board structure 43–5
  establishment 18
  expansion 21, 24–38, 48–9
  exports 35–6
  flotation 22–4, 52, 122
  Joint Chairmen 139
  privatisation 38–9, 55, 69–70
  sale 38, 55, 70, 108–9, 122
  Stage One 41–3
  Stage Three 46–55
  Stage Two 43–6
Peter Black Distribution 26, 34–5, 53–4
Peter Black Footwear & Accessories 24–8, 85
  bags 26–7
  footwear 27–8, 85
  offices in Italy and Far East 24–6
Peter Black Healthcare 35, 38, 86, 100, 121
Peter Black Holdings 44
  Non-Executive Directors 50
Peter Black Homeware 32–3, 36
Peter Black Leisurewear 28–31, 36–7
Peter Black Toiletries & Cosmetics 32, 58, 78–9, 93
philanthropy 135
Pierre Le Noir 86–7
Pilgrim Fathers 136
Player, Gary 110
politicians 81

PR
  importance 126
  targeted 89
practical jokes 73–4, 140
preparation 70, 71
price, finding optimum 88–9
product 82–91
product life cycle 142
professionalism 119–20
profitability, maintaining 79–80
publicity 119
Puma 29

quality 90, 98, 141
quantitative easing 132, 141

Red Kooga Ginseng 86
Reichstag 15–16
remuneration 117–18
Renwick, Mrs 62
retailers, and suppliers 99–100
retirement 112, 123
Robert McAlpine 47
Roman Empire 132
Ronson 27
Ross, Jonathan 126
Rothschild, Nathan 109
Rothschild 22–3, 52
The Royal Society of Midwives 73

Sabella car 20–1
saddles incident 111–12
Scholl 141
Schwarzschild, Hans *see* Black, Peter
Schwarzschild, Karl 14
Schwarzschild, Paul *see* Shields, Paul
sewing factories 68
Shakespeare, William 106
Shakeweight 126
Shields, Paul (Paul Schwarzschild) 14, 17
short-termism 100, 101
Sieff, David 25, 26
Sieff, Lord Marcus 28, 94, 97, 121
Silsden 39
slippers 18–19, 27–8
South Korea 134
speculation 123
speechmaking 71
Spitz, Mark 86
sport, and business 62–3
Springuru 85
staff welfare 98
Stevenson, Robert Louis 56
stress, work-related 104
success, formula for 144
suicide 104
suppliers, retailers and 99–100
supply and demand 131

teamwork 64–5, 67, 77
television shopping 124–5
Thatcher, Margaret 73–4, 107
The Original Factory Shop 33–4
timing 106–13, 138
Timpson, John 94
title, choosing 7
Tito, Josip Broz 132
toilets inspection 98
trade sales 51
Trades Unions 70
trainees 57–9
Trangmar, Don 78–9, 96–7
Tring 67

Uganda 101
'under-planned' 141
USA 134–8
USSR 132

venture capitalists (VCs) 51, 54–5
Vistram 42
vitamins 35
vulcanising 18–19

Waldorf Astoria 25, 26
Waller, Charlie 102, 104
Waller, Mark 102
Waller, Rachel 102

'wets' 107
Wilson, Garry 55, 124
Wood, Chris 58
work–life balance 120

XHose 126

Yardley Cosmetics 85–6
Yugoslavia 132

Zhou Enlai 111
Zilkha, Selim 27, 72